W9-BOL-992

THIMBLEBERRIES®

Quilting a
Patchwork Garden

by Lynette Jensen

Landauer Books

THIMBLEBERRIES®
Quilting a
Patchwork Garden

Copyright© 2007 by Landauer Corporation

Projects Copyright© 2007 by Lynette Jensen

This book was designed, produced, and published by Landauer Books
A division of Landauer Corporation
3100 NW 101st Street, Urbandale, Iowa 50322
www.landauercorp.com   800/557-2144

President: Jeramy Lanigan Landauer
Director of Sales & Operations: Kitty Jacobson
Editor-in-Chief: Becky Johnston
Managing Editor: Jeri Simon
Art Director: Laurel Albright
Photographer: Craig Anderson

For Thimbleberries®:
Creative Director: Lynette Jensen
Art Director: Kate Grussing
Photostyling: Lynette Jensen
Technical Writer: Sue Bahr
Technical Illustrator: Lisa Kirchoff

We also wish to thank the support staff of the Thimbleberries® Design Studio: Sherry Husske, Virginia Brodd, Renae Ashwill, Ardelle Paulson, Julie Jergens, Clarine Howe, Tracy Schrantz, Amy Albrecht, and Leone Rusch.

We extend our thanks also to Marilyn and Michael Ginsberg for sharing flowers from their beautifully maintained gardens.

The following manufacturers are licensed to sell Thimbleberries® products: Thimbleberries® Rugs (www.colonialmills.com); Thimbleberries® Quilt Stencils (www.quiltingcreations.com); Thimbleberries® Sewing Thread (www.robison-anton.com); and Thimbleberries® Fabrics (RJR Fabrics available at independent quilt shops).

This book is printed on acid-free paper.

Printed in China 10 9 8 7 6 5 4 3 2

Library of Congress Cataloging-in-Publication Data

Jensen, Lynette.
   Thimbleberries quilting a patchwork garden / by Lynette Jensen.
      p. cm.
   ISBN-13: 978-1-890621-62-9
   ISBN-10: 1-890621-62-5
   1. Patchwork--Patterns. 2. Quilting--Patterns. 3. Quilted goods. I.
Title. II. Title: Quilting a patchwork garden. III. Title: Patchwork
garden.
   TT835.J515 2007
   746.46'041--dc22
                     2006048891

ISBN 13: 978-1-890621-62-9

Foreword

My passion for quilting is almost matched by my love for gardening. As my quilt collection has grown over the years, so grows my garden!

With a busy schedule of travel and designing for Thimbleberries®, it was an easy solution to bring on "temporary" summer help for keeping the gardens looking their best. With gloves, tools, and lots of water, students, Kristin Kirchoff and Elizabeth Brodd, below, lovingly helped tend my garden and potted plants in my absence. And who knows, they may come to love gardening as much as I do.

Many of the quilts, pillows and table toppers I design for Thimbleberries® are inspired by the garden glory you'll find on the following pages. For added inspiration, I discovered the charm of vintage watering cans painted in seasonal garden colors—from soft springtime blossoms to summer sunshine and autumn harvest rust and brown. The cans served more than their original purpose as they became the color theme you'll find in the chapters that follow.

From morning light to evening glow, I sincerely hope that entertaining friends and family on your patio or porch surrounded by the soft comforts you've made by hand is as soul satisfying as it is to me.

My best,

Lynette Jensen

contents

Morning Light

Afternoon Ambience

contents

Evening Glow

Introduction

Entertaining has never been easier than with easy breezy, garden-inspired quilts and projects designed for patio, porch or even an impromptu indoor picnic.

Treat yourself to a patchwork garden of 16 quilting inspirations with a new collection of quilts, wallhangings, runners, pillows and place mats designed by Lynette Jensen for Thimbleberries®. Choose from a patchwork garden of well-loved blocks—from Daisy Chain, Tulip and Flying Geese to Paddlewheel Surround and Chevron Log Cabin— featured in quilts inspired by Lynette's glorious gardens.

From early morning through the afternoon and into the evening, delight your friends and family with quilts, pillows and table toppers that can be enjoyed indoors or outdoors. Discover the simple pleasures of surrounding yourself with memories of spring blossoms, summer sunshine and autumn harvest when you quilt your own patchwork garden that will bloom for many years to come.

Morning Light

*Start your day softly with a gentle
mix of quilts and pillows that are
perfect for early mornings on the patio.
Sip your morning coffee or share
a neighborly cup of tea with
garden-inspired easy breezy quilts
and patchwork pillows.*

Quilt

56 x 65-inches

Soft as the morning breeze, the Sage Garden Patch Quilt is a subtle blend of 18 green and beige pieced blocks surrounding a dozen rose floral center blocks.

Fabrics and Supplies

1-1/4 yards **GREEN PRINT**
for pieced blocks and inner border

1-3/4 yards **ROSE FLORAL**
for center blocks, pieced blocks,
and outer border

1-1/2 yards **BEIGE PRINT**
for alternate blocks, side
and corner triangles

5/8 yard **GREEN PRINT** for binding

3-1/2 yards for backing

Quilt batting, at least 62 x 71-inches

Before beginning this project, read through
General Instructions *on page 110.*

Pieced Blocks

Makes 18 blocks

Note: *To make the piecing easier for this block, we are using the strip piecing technique. This usually means there will be extra pieces of fabric remaining for fun small projects, or to save for pieced scrap borders. Refer to* **Hints and Helps for Pressing Strip Sets** *on page 121.*

Cutting

From **GREEN PRINT**:

- Cut 6, 2-1/2 x 42-inch strips. From the strips cut:
  36, 2-1/2 x 6-1/2-inch rectangles
- Cut 4 more 2-1/2 x 42 inch strips

From **ROSE FLORAL**:

- Cut 2, 2-1/2 x 42-inch strips

Piecing

Step 1 Aligning long edges, sew 2-1/2 x 42-inch **GREEN** strips to both side edges of the 2-1/2 x 42-inch **ROSE FLORAL** strips; press. Make a total of 2 strip sets. Cut the strip sets into segments.

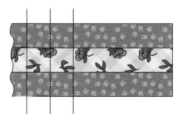

Crosscut 18, 2-1/2-inch wide segments

Step 2 Sew 2 1/2 x 6-1/2-inch **GREEN** rectangles to both side edges of the Step 1 segments; press. At this point each pieced block should measure 6-1/2-inches square.

Make 18

Quilt Center

Cutting

From **BEIGE PRINT**:

- Cut 4, 6-1/2 x 42-inch strips. From the strips cut: 20, 6-1/2-inch squares for the alternate blocks
- Cut 2, 10-1/2 x 42-inch strips. From the strips cut: 5, 10-1/2-inch squares. Cut each square twice diagonally to make 20 triangles. You will be using only 18 for side triangles. Also, cut, 2, 6-1/2-inch squares. Cut each square once diagonally to make 4 corner triangles.

10-1/2-inch squares

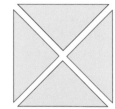

Side triangles

6-1/2-inch squares

Corner triangles

From **ROSE FLORAL**:

- Cut 2, 6-1/2 x 42-inch strips. From the strips cut: 12, 6-1/2-inch center block squares

Note: The side and corner triangles are larger than necessary and will be trimmed before the borders are added.

Quilt Center Assembly

Step 1 Referring to the quilt center assembly diagram, sew together the 18 pieced blocks, **ROSE FLORAL** center blocks, **BEIGE** alternate blocks, and **BEIGE** side triangles in 10 diagonal rows. Press the seam allowances in alternating directions by rows so the seams will fit snugly together with less bulk.

Quilt Center Assembly

Step 2 Pin the rows at the block intersections; sew the rows together. Press the seam allowances in one direction.

Step 3 Sew the **BEIGE** corner triangles to the quilt center; press.

Step 4 Trim away the excess fabric from the side and corner triangles taking care to allow a 1/4-inch seam allowance beyond the corners of each block. Refer to **Trimming Side and Corner Triangles** for complete instructions.

Trimming Side and Corner Triangles

Begin at a corner by lining up your ruler 1/4-inch beyond the points of the block corners as shown. Cut along the edge of the ruler. Repeat this procedure on all four sides of the quilt top.

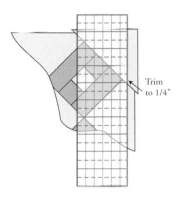

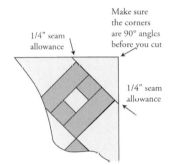

Borders

Note: The yardage given allows for the border strips to be cut on the crosswise grain. Diagonally piece the strips as needed, referring to **Diagonal Piecing** *instructions on page 123. Read through* **Border** *instructions on page 121 for general instructions on adding borders.*

Cutting

From **GREEN PRINT**:
* Cut 5, 2-1/2 x 42-inch inner border strips

From **ROSE FLORAL**:
* Cut 7, 5-1/2 x 42-inch outer border strips

Attaching the Borders

Step 1   Attach the 2-1/2-inch wide **GREEN** inner border strips.

Step 2   Attach the 5-1/2-inch wide **ROSE FLORAL** outer border strips.

Putting It All Together

Cut the 3-1/2 yard length of backing fabric in half crosswise to make 2, 1-3/4 yard lengths. Refer to **Finishing the Quilt** on page 123 for complete instructions.

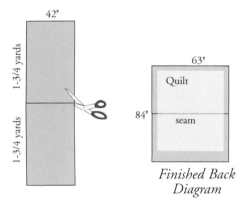

Finished Back Diagram

Quilting Suggestions:

* All quilt center blocks/squares - **TB6 Leaf Quarter**.
* Side triangles - 1/2 of **TB6 Leaf Quarter**.
* Corner triangles - 1/4 of **TB6 Leaf Quarter**.
* Inner and Outer borders quilted as one border - **TB32 Blossom Swirl**.

THIMBLEBERRIES® quilt stencils by Quilting Creations International are available at your local quilt shop.

* The quilt photographed was meandered.

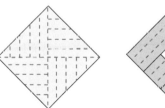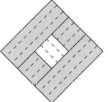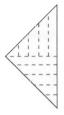

Another Quilting Suggestion

Binding

Cutting

From **GREEN PRINT**:
* Cut 7, 2-3/4 x 42-inch strips

Sew the binding to the quilt using a 3/8-inch seam allowance. This measurement will produce a 1/2-inch wide finished double binding. Refer to **Binding** and **Diagonal Piecing** instructions on page 123 for complete instructions.

Sage Garden Patch

Quilting Suggestion

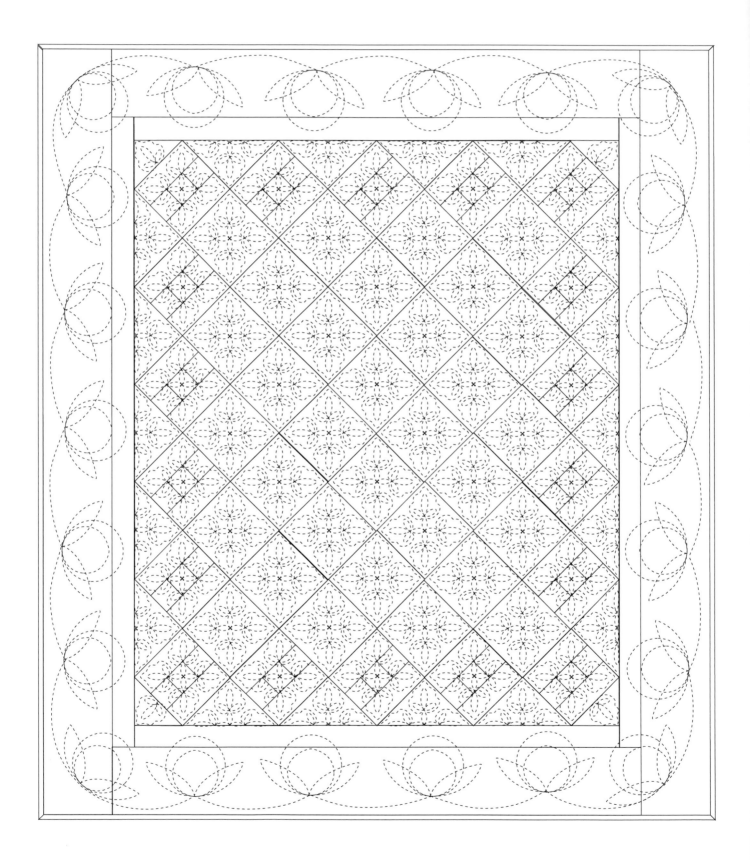

Sage Garden Patch

Quilt

56 x 65-inches

Easy Breezy

Fabrics and Supplies

Note: Yardage is based on 42-1/2-inch wide fabric. If your fabric is narrower than 42-1/2-inches you will need to adjust your measurements.

1-1/2 yards GOLD TOILE
for center square and corner squares

5/8 yard EGGPLANT PRINT
for inner border

1/3 yard ROSE PRINT
for one middle border

1/3 yard PEACH PRINT
for one middle border

1/3 yard GREEN PRINT
for one middle border

1/3 yard GOLD PRINT
for one middle border

4-3/4 yards EGGPLANT FLORAL
for outer border
(cut on the lengthwise grain)

7/8 yard EGGPLANT PRINT for binding

3 yards for 108-inch wide backing **OR**
8-2/3 yards for 42-inch wide backing

Quilt batting, at least 104-inches square

Before beginning this project, read through **General Instructions** *on page 110.*

Note: The yardage given allows for the inner and middle border strips to be cut on the crosswise grain. Diagonally piece the strips as needed, referring to **Diagonal Piecing** *on page 123.*

Quilt

98-inches square

For a light and airy table covering, start with a gold toile center square that measures a generous 42-inches. Simply add corner squares and inner and outer borders for an Easy Breezy Quilt.

Center Block

Cutting

From **GOLD TOILE**:
- Cut 1, 42-1/2-inch square
- Cut 4, 8-1/2-inch squares

From **EGGPLANT PRINT**:
- Cut 7, 2-1/2 x 42-inch strips. From the strips cut:
  2, 2-1/2 x 62-1/2-inch strips
  2, 2-1/2 x 42-1/2-inch strips
  4, 2-1/2 x 8 1/2-inch strips

From **ROSE PRINT** and **PEACH PRINT**:
- Cut 1, 8-1/2 x 42-1/2-inch strip from each

From **GREEN PRINT** and **GOLD PRINT**:
- Cut 1, 8-1/2 x 42-1/2-inch strip from each

Piecing

Step 1 Sew a 2-1/2 x 42-1/2-inch **EGGPLANT** strip to the top/bottom edges of the 42-1/2-inch **GOLD TOILE** square; press. Sew the 8-1/2 x 42-1/2-inch **GREEN** and **GOLD PRINT** strips to the top/bottom edges of this unit; press.

Step 2 Sew 2-1/2 x 62-1/2-inch **EGGPLANT** strips to both side edges of the quilt center; press.

Step 3 Sew 2-1/2 x 8-1/2-inch **EGGPLANT** strips to both ends of the **ROSE** and **PEACH PRINT** strips; press. Sew 8-1/2-inch **GOLD TOILE** squares to both ends of the strips; press. Sew the strips to both side edges of the quilt center; press. At this point the quilt center should measure 62-1/2-inches square.

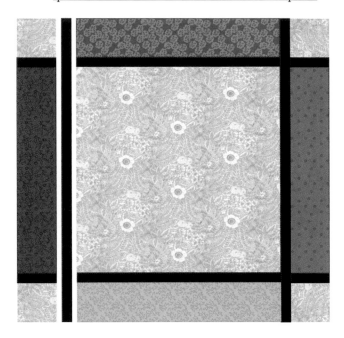

Outer Border

Note: *The yardage given allows for the outer border strips to be cut on the lengthwise grain. A few extra inches have been allowed for trimming. Read through **Border** instructions on page 121 for general instructions on adding borders.*

Cutting

From **EGGPLANT FLORAL**:

(cut on the lengthwise grain)

• Cut 2, 18-1/2 x 100-inches
• Cut 2, 18-1/2 x 65-inches

Attaching the Outer Border

Step 1 Attach the 18-1/2 x 65-inch **EGGPLANT FLORAL** border strips to the top/bottom edges of the quilt top; press. Trim the strips as needed.

Step 2 Attach the 18-1/2 x 100-inch **EGGPLANT FLORAL** border strips to the side edges of the quilt top; press. Trim the strips as needed.

Putting It All Together

Step 1 If you are using 108-inch wide backing fabric, simply trim the backing and batting so they are 3-inches larger on each side than the quilt top.

Note: *If you are using 42-inch wide backing fabric, cut the 8-2/3 yard length of 42-inch wide backing fabric in thirds crosswise to make 3, 2-7/8 yard lengths. Sew the long edges together; press. Trim the backing and batting so they are 3-inches larger on each side than the quilt top.*

Step 2 Refer to **Finishing the Quilt** on page 123 for complete instructions.

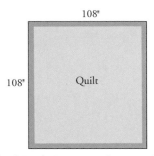

Finished Back Diagram (108-inch wide fabric)

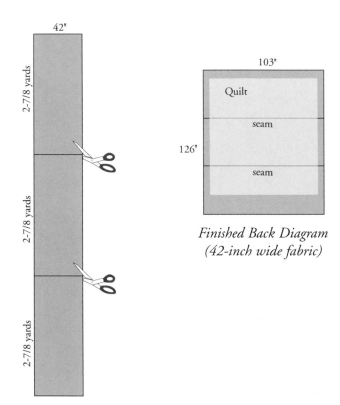

Finished Back Diagram (42-inch wide fabric)

Binding

Cutting

From **EGGPLANT PRINT**:

- Cut 10, 2-3/4 x 42-inch strips

Sew the binding to the quilt using a 3/8-inch seam allowance. This measurement will produce a 1/2-inch wide finished double binding. Refer to **Binding** and **Diagonal Piecing** on page 123 for complete instructions.

Easy Breezy

Quilt

98-inches square

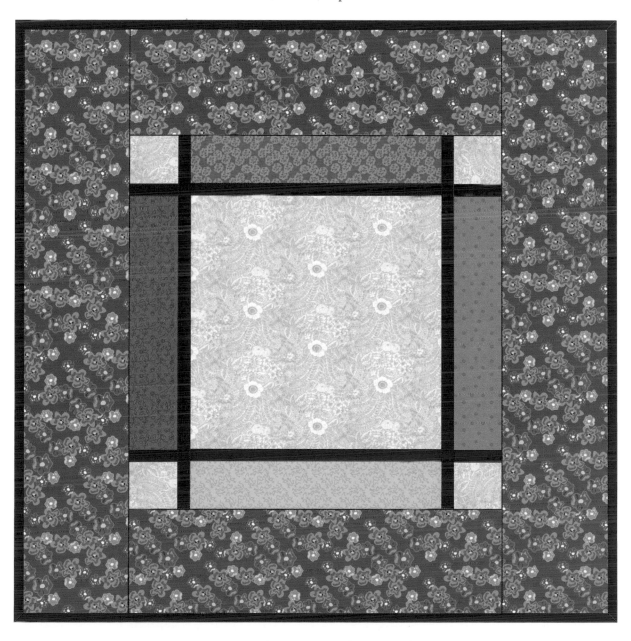

Easy Breezy Pillow

22-inches square

For a fast-finish pillow with extra dimension, first attach a ruffle to a band of striped fabric that complements the floral top and back of this Easy Breezy Pillow.

Fabrics and Supplies

1-3/4 yards **TAN FLORAL** for pillow top (lower section) and pillow back

1/4 yard **WIDE TAN STRIPE** for pillow top (upper band)

1/3 yard **NARROW TAN STRIPE** for ruffle

22-inch square pillow form

Before beginning this project, read through **General Instructions** *on page 110.*

Pillow Top and Ruffle

Cutting

From **TAN FLORAL**:
  • Cut 1, 16 x 23-inch rectangle for lower section

From **WIDE TAN STRIPE**:
  • Cut 1, 8 x 23-inch rectangle for upper band

From **NARROW TAN STRIPE**:
  • Cut 2, 5 x 42-inch strips for the ruffle

Attaching the Ruffle

Step 1   Piece the 5 x 42-inch **NARROW TAN STRIPE** ruffle strips together end-to-end; press. Trim the strip to 55-inches long. Fold the strip in half lengthwise, wrong sides together; press. Mark the center point of the ruffle strip with a safety pin.

Step 2   To gather the ruffle, position a heavy thread 1/4-inch in from the raw edges of the ruffle strip. You will need a length of thread 55-inches long.

Secure one end of the thread by stitching across it. Zigzag stitch over the thread the length of the strip, taking care not to sew through it.

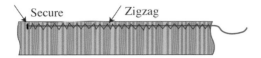

Step 3 Divide the upper edge (23-inch side) of the **TAN FLORAL** rectangle in half; mark. With raw edges aligned and center points matching, pin the prepared ruffle to the upper edge of the **TAN FLORAL** rectangle. Pull up the gathering stitches until the ruffle fits the pillow front. Machine baste the ruffle in place using a 1/4-inch seam allowance. (Any basting stitches that show will be removed in Step 4.)

Step 4 With right sides together, position the 8 x 23-inch **WIDE TAN STRIPE** rectangle at the upper edge of the **TAN FLORAL** rectangle. The ruffle will be sandwiched between the 2 layers and turned toward the **TAN FLORAL** rectangle. Pin and stitch the pieces together using a 1/2-inch seam allowance. Press the seam allowances toward the **WIDE TAN STRIPE** rectangle. Remove any gathering stitches that show. At this point the pillow top should measure 23-inches square.

Make 1

Pillow Back

Cutting

From **TAN FLORAL**:

- Cut 2, 23 x 30-inch pillow back rectangles

Assembling the Pillow Back

Step 1 With wrong sides together, fold each **TAN FLORAL** pillow back rectangle in half crosswise to make 2, 15 x 23-inch double-thick pillow back pieces. Overlap the 2 folded edges so the pillow back measures 23-inches square. Pin the pieces together and machine baste around the entire piece to create a single pillow back, using a 3/8-inch seam allowance. The double thickness of the pillow back will make it more stable and give it a nice finishing touch.

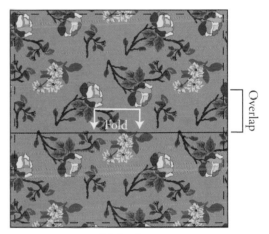

Make 1

Step 2 With right sides together, layer the pillow back and the pillow top; pin. Stitch around the outside edges using a 1/2-inch seam allowance. Turn the pillow right side out and insert the pillow form through the back opening.

Broken Dishes
Pillow

20-inches square without ruffle

*Patch up a pillow in no time at all with
four horizontal rows of triangle-pieced
squares that make up the pieced block known
to generations of quilters as Broken Dishes.*

Fabrics and Supplies

1/4 yard **BLUE PRINT** for block

1/4 yard **BEIGE PRINT**
for block background

1/4 yard **GOLD PRINT**
for inner border

2-1/8 yards **GREEN FLORAL** for outer
border, ruffle, and pillow back

5/8 yard muslin lining
for quilted pillow top

Quilt batting, at least 22-inches square

20-inch square pillow form

Before beginning this project, read through
***General Instructions** on page 110.*

Pieced Block

Cutting

From **BLUE PRINT**:

- Cut 1, 3-7/8 x 42-inch strip

From **BEIGE PRINT**:

- Cut 1, 3-7/8 x 42-inch strip

Piecing

Step 1 With right sides together, layer together the
3-7/8 x 42-inch **BLUE** and **BEIGE** strips. Press
together, but do not sew. Cut the layered strips into
squares. Cut the layered squares in half diagonally to
make 16 sets of triangles. Stitch 1/4-inch from the
diagonal edge of each set of triangles; press. At this
point each triangle-pieced square should measure
3-1/2-inches square.

Crosscut 8, 3-7/8-inch squares

*Make 16,
3-1/2-inch
triangle-pieced squares*

Step 2 Sew the triangle-pieced squares together in 4
horizontal rows. Press the seam allowances in
alternating directions by rows so the seams will fit
snugly together with less bulk. Sew the rows
together; press. At this point the block should
measure 12-1/2-inches square.

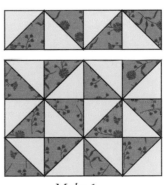

Make 1

Borders

Cutting

From **GOLD PRINT**:

- Cut 2, 2-1/2 x 42-inch inner border strips

From **GREEN FLORAL**:

- Cut 2, 2-1/2 x 42-inch outer border strips

Attaching the Borders

Step 1 Attach the 2-1/2-inch wide **GOLD** inner border strips.

Step 2 Attach the 2-1/2-inch wide **GREEN FLORAL** outer border strips.

Putting It All Together

Cutting

From muslin lining and batting:

- Cut 1, 22-inch square from each

Assembly

Step 1 Layer the 22-inch muslin lining square, batting, and pieced pillow top. Hand baste the layers together; quilt as desired. When quilting is complete, trim the excess backing and batting even with the pillow top.

Step 2 To prepare the pillow top before attaching the ruffle, we suggest hand basting the edges of all 3 layers of the pillow top together. This will prevent the edge of the pillow top from rippling when you attach the ruffle.

Pillow Ruffle

Cutting

From **GREEN FLORAL**:

- Cut 6, 6-3/4 x 42-inch strips

Attaching the Ruffle

Step 1 Diagonally piece the 6-3/4-inch wide **GREEN FLORAL** strips together to make a continuous ruffle strip, referring to *Diagonal Piecing* on page 123 for instructions.

Step 2 Fold the strip in half lengthwise, wrong sides together; press. Divide the ruffle strip into 4 equal segments; mark the quarter points with safety pins.

Step 3 To gather the ruffle, position quilting thread (or 2 strands of regular-weight sewing thread) 1/4-inch from the raw edges of the ruffle. You will need a length of thread 200-inches long. Secure one end of the thread by stitching across it. Zigzag stitch over the thread all the way around the ruffle, taking care not to sew through it.

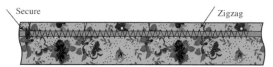

Secure   Zigzag

Step 4 Divide the edges of the pillow top into 4 equal segments; mark the quarter points with safety pins. With right sides together and raw edges aligned, pin the ruffle to the pillow top, matching the quarter points. Pull up the gathering stitches until the ruffle fits the pillow top, taking care to allow extra fullness in the ruffle at each corner. Sew the ruffle to the pillow top, using a 1/4-inch seam allowance.

Pillow Back

Cutting

From **GREEN FLORAL**

• Cut 2, 20-1/2 x 28-inch rectangles

Assembling the Pillow Back

Step 1 With wrong sides together, fold each 20-1/2 x 28-inch rectangle in half crosswise to make 2, 14 x 20-1/2-inch double-thick pillow back pieces. Overlap the 2 folded edges so the pillow back measures 20-1/2-inches square; pin. Pin the pieces together and machine baste around the entire piece to create a single pillow back using a 1/4-inch seam allowance. The double thickness of the pillow back will make it more stable and give it a nice finishing touch.

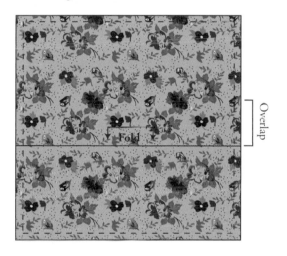

Step 2 With right sides together, layer the pillow back and the quilted pillow top; pin. The ruffle will be sandwiched between the 2 layers and turned toward the center of the pillow at this time. Pin and stitch around the outside edges using a 3/8-inch seam allowance.

Step 3 Trim the pillow back and corner seam allowances if needed. Turn the pillow right side out, insert the pillow form through the back opening, and fluff up the ruffle.

Maple Leaf
Pillow

20-inches square without ruffle

*A study in serenity, a solo leaf block
with appliqué stem and leaves takes
center stage on this
handsome Maple Leaf Pillow.*

Fabrics and Supplies

1/3 yard **GREEN PRINT** for leaf block

1/4 yard **CREAM PRINT**
for block background

1/4 yard **ROSE PRINT** for inner border

2-1/8 yards **GREEN FLORAL**
for outer border, ruffle, and pillow back

5/8 yard muslin lining
for quilted pillow top

Quilt batting, at least 22-inches square

20-inch square pillow form

8-inch square freezer paper for appliqués

Before beginning this project, read through
General Instructions *on page 110.*

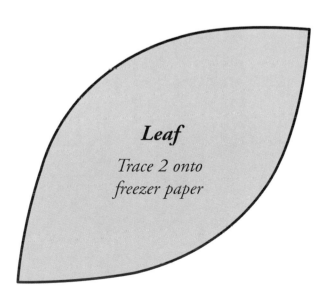

Leaf

Trace 2 onto
freezer paper

Pieced Block

Cutting

From **GREEN PRINT**:

- Cut 1, 1-3/4 x 8-inch **bias** strip.

From the remaining fabric:

- Cut 2, 3-1/2 x 28-inch strips. From the strips cut:

  1, 3-1/2 x 12-1/2-inch rectangle

  2, 3-1/2 x 6-1/2-inch rectangles

  2, 3-1/2-inch squares

From **CREAM PRINT**:

- Cut 2, 3-1/2 x 42-inch strips. From the strips cut:

  1, 3-1/2 x 12-1/2-inch rectangle

  1, 3-1/2 x 6-1/2-inch rectangle

  8, 3-1/2-inch squares

Piecing

Step 1 With right sides together, position a
3-1/2-inch **GREEN** square on the corner
of a 3-1/2 x 6 1/2-inch **CREAM** rectangle.
Draw a diagonal line on the square and stitch on
the line. Trim the seam allowance to 1/4-inch;
press. Repeat this process at the opposite corner of
the rectangle. Sew a 3-1/2-inch **CREAM** square to
both ends of the unit; press. <u>At this point the unit
should measure 3-1/2 x 12-1/2-inches.</u>

Make 1

Step 2 With right sides together, position 3-1/2-inch
CREAM squares on both corners of the
3-1/2 x 12-1/2-inch **GREEN** rectangle. Draw
a diagonal line on the squares; stitch, trim, and
press. <u>At this point the unit should measure
3-1/2 x 12-1/2-inches.</u>

Make 1

Step 3 With right sides together, position a 3-1/2-inch **CREAM** square on the corner of a 3-1/2 x 6-1/2-inch **GREEN** rectangle. Draw a diagonal line on the square; stitch, trim, and press. Repeat this process at the opposite corner of the rectangle. Make another unit reversing the direction of the stitching lines. Sew the 2 units together; press. Sew a 3-1/2 x 12-1/2-inch **CREAM** rectangle to the bottom edge of the unit; press. <u>At this point the unit should measure 6-1/2 x 12-1/2-inches.</u>

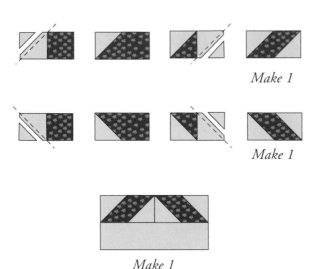

Make 1

Make 1

Make 1

Step 4 To prepare the stem appliqué, fold the 1-3/4 x 8-inch **GREEN** strip in half lengthwise with wrong sides together; press. Stitch a scant 1/4-inch from the raw edges to keep them aligned. Fold the strip in half lengthwise so the raw edges are hidden by the first folded edge; press. Position the stem strip on the Step 3 unit. Appliqué the stem in place with matching thread.

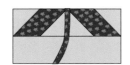

Make 1

Step 5 Make a template using the leaf shape on page 31. Trace the shape on the paper side of the freezer paper; cut out the shapes on the traced lines. Press the coated side of each freezer paper shape onto the wrong side of the fabric chosen for the appliqué. (Allow at least 1/2-inch between each shape for seam allowances.) Cut out each shape a scant 1/4-inch beyond the edge of the freezer paper pattern.

Step 6 Position the leaves on the Step 4 unit. With your needle, turn the seam allowance over the edge of the freezer paper; appliqué the shape in place with matching thread. When there is about 3/4-inch left to appliqué, slide your needle into this opening, loosen the freezer paper from the fabric, and gently pull the freezer paper out. Finish stitching the appliqué in place. Repeat with the remaining shape.

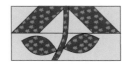

Make 1

Step 7 Sew the Step 1, Step 2, and Step 6 units together to complete the block; press. <u>At this point the leaf block should measure 12-1/2-inches square.</u>

Make 1

Borders

Note: *Read through* ***Border*** *instructions on page 121 for general instructions on adding borders.*

Cutting

From **ROSE PRINT**:

• Cut 2, 2-1/2 x 42-inch inner border strips

From **GREEN FLORAL**:

• Cut 2, 2-1/2 x 42-inch outer border strips

Attaching the Borders

Step 1 Attach the 2-1/2-inch wide **ROSE** inner border strips.

Step 2 Attach the 2-1/2-inch wide **GREEN FLORAL** outer border strips.

Putting It All Together

Cutting

From muslin lining and batting:
- Cut 1, 22-inch square from each

Assembly

Step 1 Layer the 22-inch muslin lining square, batting, and pieced pillow top. Hand baste the layers together; quilt as desired. When quilting is complete, trim the excess backing and batting even with the pillow top.

Step 2 To prepare the pillow top before attaching the ruffle, we suggest hand basting the edges of all 3 layers of the pillow top together. This will prevent the edge of the pillow top from rippling when you attach the ruffle.

Pillow Ruffle

Cutting

From **GREEN FLORAL**:
- Cut 6, 6-3/4 x 42-inch strips

Attaching the Ruffle

Step 1 Diagonally piece the 6 3/4 inch wide **GREEN FLORAL** strips together to make a continuous ruffle strip, referring to **Diagonal Piecing** on page 123 for instructions.

Step 2 Fold the strip in half lengthwise, wrong sides together; press. Divide the ruffle strip into 4 equal segments; mark the quarter points with safety pins.

Step 3 To gather the ruffle, position quilting thread (or 2 strands of regular-weight sewing thread) 1/4-inch from the raw edges of the ruffle. You will need a length of thread 200-inches long. Secure one end of the thread by stitching across it. Zigzag stitch over the thread all the way around the ruffle, taking care not to sew through it.

Step 4 Divide the edges of the pillow top into 4 equal segments; mark the quarter points with safety pins. With right sides together and raw edges aligned, pin the ruffle to the pillow top, matching the quarter points. Pull up the gathering stitches until the ruffle fits the pillow top, taking care to allow extra fullness in the ruffle at each corner. Sew the ruffle to the pillow top, using a 1/4-inch seam allowance.

Pillow Back

Cutting

From **GREEN FLORAL**:
- Cut 2, 20-1/2 x 28-inch rectangles

Assembling the Pillow Back

Step 1 With wrong sides together, fold each 20-1/2 x 28-inch rectangle in half crosswise to make 2, 14 x 20-1/2-inch double-thick pillow back pieces. Overlap the 2 folded edges so the pillow back measures 20-1/2-inches square; pin. Pin the pieces together and machine baste around the entire piece to create a single pillow back using a 1/4-inch seam allowance. The double thickness of the pillow back will make it more stable and give it a nice finishing touch.

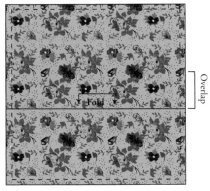

Step 2 With right sides together, layer the pillow back and the quilted pillow top; pin. The ruffle will be sandwiched between the 2 layers and turned toward the center of the pillow at this time. Pin and stitch around the outside edges using a 3/8-inch seam allowance.

Step 3 Trim the pillow back and corner seam allowances if needed. Turn the pillow right side out, insert the pillow form through the back opening, and fluff up the ruffle.

Daisy Chain

Quilt

87 x 105-inches

Wake up as fresh as the proverbial daisy with Nine-Patch blocks cleverly pieced together to create this surprisingly simple Daisy Chain Quilt.

Fabrics and Supplies

2 yards **ROSE PRINT** for blocks

1/4 yard **GOLD PRINT** for blocks

2-5/8 yards **BEIGE PRINT** for background

4-1/8 yards **GREEN PRINT** for alternate blocks and outer border

1 yard **BLUE PRINT** for inner border

7/8 yard **BLUE PRINT** for binding

8 yards for backing

Quilt batting, at least 93 x 111-inches

*Before beginning this project, read through **General Instructions** on page 110.*

9-Patch Blocks

Makes 14 blocks

Cutting

From **ROSE PRINT**:

- Cut 7, 3-1/2 x 42-inch strips

From **GOLD PRINT**:

- Cut 2, 3-1/2 x 42-inch strips

From **BEIGE PRINT**:

- Cut 6, 3-1/2 x 42-inch strips

Piecing

Step 1 Aligning long edges, sew 3-1/2 x 42-inch **ROSE** strips to both side edges of a 3-1/2 x 42-inch **GOLD** strip. Make 2 strip sets. Press the strip sets referring to *Hints and Helps for Pressing Strip Sets*. Cut the strip sets into segments.

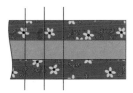

Crosscut 14, 3-1/2-inch wide segments

Hints and Helps for Pressing Strip Sets

When sewing strips of fabric together for strip sets, it is important to press the seam allowances nice and flat, usually to the dark fabric. Be careful not to stretch as you press, causing a "rainbow effect." This will affect the accuracy and shape of the pieces cut from the strip set. Press on the wrong side first with the strips perpendicular to the ironing board. Flip the piece over and press on the right side to prevent little pleats from forming at the seams. Laying the strip set lengthwise on the ironing board seems to encourage the rainbow effect.

Avoid this rainbow effect

Step 2 Aligning long edges, sew 3-1/2 x 42-inch **BEIGE** strips to both side edges of a 3-1/2 x 42-inch **ROSE** strip. Make 3 strip sets; press. Cut the strip sets into segments.

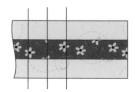

Crosscut 28, 3-1/2-inch wide segments

Step 3 Sew the Step 2 units to the top/bottom edges of the Step 1 units; press. <u>At this point each 9-patch block should measure 9-1/2-inches square.</u>

Make 14

Pieced Blocks

Makes 31 blocks

Cutting

From **ROSE PRINT**:
- Cut 7, 3-7/8 x 42-inch strips
- Cut 3, 3-1/2 x 42-inch strips

From **BEIGE PRINT**:
- Cut 7, 3-7/8 x 42-inch strips
- Cut 6, 3-1/2 x 42-inch strips
- Cut 6 more 3-1/2 x 42-inch strips.
  From the strips cut:
  62, 3-1/2-inch squares

Piecing

Step 1 Aligning long edges, sew 3-1/2 x 42-inch **BEIGE** strips to both side edges of a 3-1/2 x 42-inch **ROSE** strip. Make 3 strip sets; press. Cut the strip sets into segments.

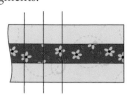

Crosscut 31, 3-1/2-inch wide segments

Step 2 With right sides together, layer the 3-7/8 x 42-inch **ROSE** and **BEIGE** strips in pairs. Press together, but do not sew. Cut the layered strips into squares. Cut the layered squares in half diagonally to make 124 sets of triangles. Stitch 1/4-inch from the diagonal edge of each pair of triangles; press.

Crosscut 62, 3-7/8-inch wide segments

*Make 124,
3-1/2-inch
triangle-pieced squares*

Step 3 Sew Step 2 triangle-pieced squares to both side edges of a 3-1/2-inch **BEIGE** square; press.

Make 62

Step 4 Sew the Step 3 units to the top/bottom edges of the Step 1 units; press. <u>At this point each pieced block should measure 9-1/2-inches square.</u>

Make 31

Quilt Center

Cutting

From **GREEN PRINT**:
- Cut 5, 9-1/2 x 42-inch strips. From the strips cut: 18, 9-1/2-inch alternate block squares

Quilt Center Assembly

Step 1 Referring to the quilt diagram for placement, lay out the 9-patch blocks, pieced blocks, and alternate blocks in 9 rows with 7 blocks in each row.

Step 2 Sew the blocks together in each row. Press the seam allowances in alternating directions by rows so the seams will fit snugly together with less bulk. <u>At this point each block row should measure 9-1/2 x 63-1/2-inches.</u>

Step 3 Pin the rows together at the block intersections; stitch and press. <u>At this point the quilt center should measure 63-1/2 x 81-1/2-inches.</u>

Borders

*Note: The yardage given allows for the border strips to be cut on the crosswise grain. Diagonally piece the strips as needed, referring to **Diagonal Piecing** on page 123. Read through **Border** instructions on page 121 for general instructions on adding borders.*

Cutting

From **BLUE PRINT**:

• Cut 9, 3-1/2 x 42-inch inner border strips

From **GREEN PRINT**:

• Cut 10, 9-1/2 x 42-inch outer border strips

Attaching the Borders

Step 1 Attach the 3-1/2-inch wide **BLUE** inner border strips.

Step 2 Attach the 9-1/2-inch wide **GREEN** outer border strips.

Putting It All Together

Cut the 8 yard length of backing fabric in thirds crosswise to make 3, 2-2/3 yard lengths. Refer to *Finishing the Quilt* on page 123 for complete instructions.

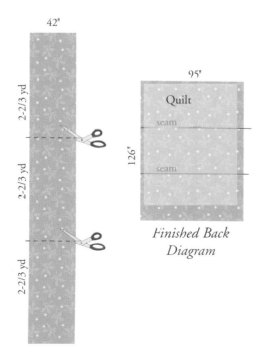

Finished Back Diagram

Quilting Suggestions:

• 9-Patch blocks - **TB21 Tulip**.
• Pieced blocks - **TB7 Leaf Quartet**.
• **GREEN** alternate blocks - **TB24 Floral Burst**.
• **BLUE** inner border - **TB27 Heart Vine Border**.
• **GREEN** outer border - **TB38 Pansy Vine**.

THIMBLEBERRIES® *quilt stencils by Quilting Creations International are available at your local quilt shop.*

• The quilt photographed was meandered.

Binding

Cutting

From **BLUE PRINT**:

• Cut 10, 2-3/4 x 42-inch strips

Sew the binding to the quilt using a 3/8-inch seam allowance. This measurement will produce a 1/2-inch wide finished double binding. Refer to **Binding** and **Diagonal Piecing** on page 123 for complete instructions.

Daisy Chain

Quilting Suggestion

Daisy Chain

Quilt

87 x 105-inches

Tulip Patch

Wall Quilt

50 x 56-inches

Brighten your day nine times over with a burst of blooms pieced together to make this cheery Tulip Patch Wall Quilt.

Fabrics and Supplies

1/2 yard **PEACH PRINT**
for tulips and lattice posts/corner squares

1/4 yard **PEACH FLORAL** for tulips

7/8 yard **BEIGE PRINT**
for block background

3/4 yard **GREEN PRINT**
for leaves and middle border

2/3 yard **YELLOW PRINT**
for lattice segments and inner border

1 yard **LARGE AQUA FLORAL**
for outer border

5/8 yard **GREEN PRINT** for binding

3-1/4 yards for backing

Quilt batting, at least 56 x 62-inches

Before beginning this project, read through
General Instructions *on page 110.*

Blocks

Makes 9 blocks

Cutting

From **PEACH PRINT**:
- Cut 4, 2-1/2 x 42-inch strips. From the strips cut:
  18, 2-1/2 x 6-1/2-inch rectangles
  9, 2-1/2-inch squares

From **PEACH FLORAL**:
- Cut 2, 2-1/2 x 42-inch strips. From the strips cut:
  9, 2-1/2 x 6-1/2-inch rectangles

From **BEIGE PRINT**:
- Cut 11, 2-1/2 x 42-inch strips. From the strips cut:
  18, 2-1/2 x 6-1/2-inch rectangles
  18, 2-1/2 x 4-1/2-inch rectangles
  81, 2-1/2-inch squares

From **GREEN PRINT**:
- Cut 2, 4-1/2 x 42-inch strips. From the strips cut:
  18, 4-1/2-inch squares
- Cut 2, 2-1/2 x 42-inch strips. From the strips cut:
  9, 2-1/2 x 6-1/2-inch rectangles

Piecing

Step 1   With right sides together, position a 2-1/2-inch **BEIGE** square on both corners of a 2-1/2 x 6-1/2-inch **PEACH PRINT** rectangle. Draw a diagonal line on the squares and stitch on the lines. Trim the seam allowances to 1/4-inch; press.

Make 9

Make 9

Step 2 With right sides together, position a 2-1/2-inch **PEACH PRINT** square on the left corner of a 2-1/2 x 6-1/2-inch **PEACH FLORAL** rectangle. Draw a diagonal line on the square; stitch, trim, and press. Repeat this process at the opposite corner of the rectangle using a 2-1/2-inch **BEIGE** square.

Make 9

Step 3 Sew the Step 1 and Step 2 units together; press. Sew 2-1/2 x 6-1/2-inch **BEIGE** rectangles to both side edges of the units; press. At this point each tulip top unit should measure 6-1/2 x10-1/2-inches.

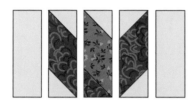

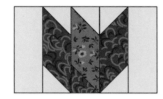

Make 9

Step 4 With right sides together, position 2-1/2-inch **BEIGE** squares on opposite corners of a 4-1/2-inch **GREEN** square. Draw a diagonal line on the squares; stitch, trim, and press.

Make 18

Step 5 Sew a 2-1/2 x 4-1/2-inch **BEIGE** rectangle to the top edge of the Step 4 units; press. Sew the units to both side edges of the 2-1/2 x 6-1/2-inch **GREEN** rectangles; press. At this point each leaf base unit should measure 6-1/2 x 10-1/2-inches.

Make 9

Step 6 Sew together the tulip top units and the leaf base units; press. At this point each block should measure 10-1/2 x 12-1/2-inches.

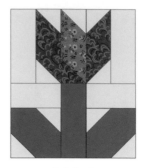

Make 9

Quilt Center

Cutting

From **YELLOW PRINT**:
- Cut 4, 2-1/2 x 42-inch strips. From the strips cut:
  6, 2-1/2 x 12-1/2-inch lattice segments
  6, 2-1/2 x 10-1/2-inch lattice segments

From **PEACH PRINT**:
- Cut 1, 2-1/2 x 42-inch strip. From the strip cut:
  8, 2-1/2-inch lattice post squares
  Set 4 aside to be used for corner squares.

Quilt Center Assembly

Step 1 Sew together 3 tulip blocks and 2 of the 2-1/2 x 12-1/2-inch **YELLOW** lattice segments. Press the seam allowances toward the lattice segments. Make 3 block rows. At this point each block row should measure 12-1/2 x 34-1/2-inches.

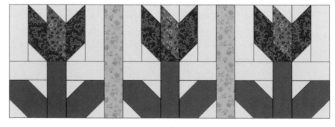

Make 3 block rows

Step 2 Sew together 3 of the 2-1/2 x 10-1/2-inch **YELLOW** lattice segments and 2 of the 2-1/2-inch **PEACH PRINT** lattice post squares. Press the seam allowances toward the lattice segments. Make 2 lattice strips. At this point each lattice strip should measure 2-1/2 x 34-1/2-inches.

Make 2 lattice strips

Step 3 Pin the block rows and lattice strips together at the block intersections and sew them together; press. At this point the quilt center should measure 34-1/2 x 40-1/2-inches.

Borders

Note: *The yardage given allows for the border strips to be cut on the crosswise grain. Diagonally piece the strips as needed, referring to* **Diagonal Piecing** *instructions on page 123. Read through* **Border** *instructions on page 121 for general instructions on adding borders.*

Cutting

From **YELLOW PRINT**:
• Cut 4, 2-1/2 x 42-inch inner border strips

From **GREEN PRINT**:
• Cut 5, 1-1/2 x 42-inch middle border strips

From **LARGE AQUA FLORAL**:
• Cut 5, 5-1/2 x 42-inch outer border strips

The 2-1/2-inch **PEACH PRINT** corner squares were cut previously.

Attaching the Borders

Step 1 Attach the 2-1/2-inch wide **YELLOW** top/bottom inner border strips; press. For the side borders, measure just the quilt top, including the seam allowances, but not the top/bottom borders. Cut the 2-1/2-inch wide **YELLOW** side inner border strips to this length. Sew a 2-1/2-inch **PEACH PRINT** corner square to both ends of the border strips; press. Sew the border strips to the side edges of the quilt center; press.

Step 2 Attach the 1-1/2-inch wide **GREEN** middle border strips.

Step 3 Attach the 5-1/2-inch wide **LARGE AQUA FLORAL** outer border strips.

Putting It All Together

Cut the 3-1/4 yard length of backing fabric in half crosswise to make 2, 1-5/8 yard lengths. Refer to **Finishing the Quilt** on page 123 for complete instructions.

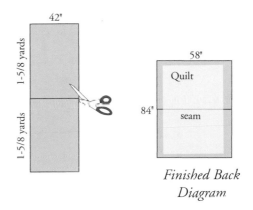

Finished Back Diagram

Quilting Suggestions:

• Tulips and leaves - echo quilting.
• **YELLOW** lattice and inner border - **TB30 Beadwork**.
• **LARGE AQUA FLORAL** outer border - **TB37 Pansy Vine**.

THIMBLEBERRIES® *quilt stencils by Quilting Creations International are available at your local quilt shop.*

Binding

Cutting

From **GREEN PRINT**:
• Cut 6, 2-3/4 x 42-inch strips

Sew the binding to the quilt using a 3/8-inch seam allowance. This measurement will produce a 1/2-inch wide finished double binding. Refer to **Binding** and **Diagonal Piecing** on page 123 for complete instructions.

Tulip Patch

Quilting Suggestion

Tulip Patch

Wall Quilt

50 x 56-inches

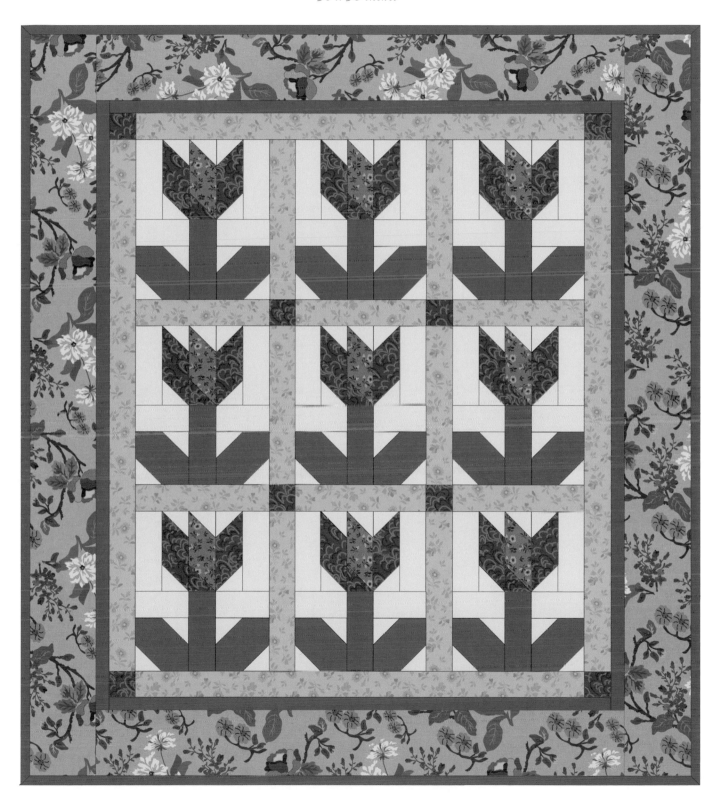

Afternoon Ambience

*What could be more relaxing than a
picnic on the patio or the porch
with plenty of patchwork?
Choose from a cheerful mix—
from the Melon Patch Place Mats
shown here to a Picnic Stars Quilt
and a Summertime Runner.*

Melon Patch

For a picnic on the porch, watermelon place mats will be the pick of the patch. And what is a melon without seeds? Seed appliqué shapes are blanket stitched in place on the melon blocks.

Fabrics and Supplies for 4 place mats

5/8 yard **BEIGE PRINT** for background and borders

1/3 yard **GREEN PRINT** for watermelon rinds

1/3 yard **RED PRINT** for watermelons

2 x 18-inch rectangle **BROWN PRINT** for seed appliqués

5/8 yard **GREEN DIAGONAL PRINT** for bindings

4 rectangles of backing fabric 16 x 22-inches each

4 rectangles of quilt batting, at least 16 x 22-inches each

Paper-backed fusible web for appliqués

Pearl cotton for decorative stitches: black

Before beginning this project, read through **General Instructions** *on page 110.*

Place Mats

12 x 18-inches

Watermelon Blocks

Makes 4 blocks

Cutting

From **BEIGE PRINT:**
- Cut 4, 2-7/8-inch squares

From **GREEN PRINT:**
- Cut 1, 2-1/2 x 42-inch strip. From the strip cut: 16, 2-1/2-inch squares

- Cut 3, 1-1/2 x 42-inch strips. From the strips cut:
  8, 1-1/2 x 6-1/2-inch rectangles
  4, 1-1/2 x 8-1/2-inch rectangles
- Cut 4, 2-7/8-inch squares

From **RED PRINT:**
- Cut 1, 6-1/2 x 42-inch strip. From the strip cut:
  4, 6-1/2 x 10-1/2-inch rectangles

- Cut 1, 1-1/2 x 42-inch strip. From the strip cut:
  4, 1-1/2 x 8-1/2-inch rectangles

Piecing

Step 1 Sew a 1-1/2 x 6-1/2-inch **GREEN** rectangle to both side edges of a 6-1/2 x 10-1/2-inch **RED** rectangle; press. Position 2-1/2-inch **GREEN** squares on the adjacent lower corners of this unit. Draw a diagonal line on the squares and stitch on the line. Trim the seam allowances to 1/4-inch; press. <u>At this point each unit should measure 6-1/2 x 12-1/2-inches.</u>

Make 4

Step 2 Sew together the 1-1/2 x 8-1/2-inch **RED** and **GREEN** rectangles in pairs; press. Position 2-1/2-inch **GREEN** squares on both corners of the unit. Draw a diagonal line on the squares; stitch, trim, and press.

Make 4

Step 3 With right sides together, layer the 2-7/8-inch **BEIGE** and **GREEN** squares in pairs. Press together, but do not sew. Cut the layered squares in half diagonally to make 8 sets of triangles. Stitch 1/4-inch from the diagonal edge of each pair of triangles; press. <u>At this point each triangle-pieced square should measure 2-1/2-inches square.</u>

Make 8, 2-1/2-inch triangle-pieced squares

Step 4 Sew triangle-pieced squares to both side edges of the Step 2 units; press. <u>At this point each unit should measure 2-1/2 x 12-1/2-inches.</u>

Make 4

Step 5 Sew together the Step 1 and Step 4 units; press. <u>At this point the watermelon block should measure 8-1/2 x 12-1/2-inches.</u>

Make 4

Fusible Web Appliqué Method

Prepare the Appliqués

Step 1 Make a seed template. Trace the shape on the paper side of the fusible web, leaving a small margin between each shape. Cut the shapes apart.

Step 2 Following the manufacturer's instructions, fuse the shapes to the wrong side of the fabric chosen for the appliqués. Let the fabric cool and cut along the traced line. Peel away the paper backing from the fusible web.

Step 3 Position the seed appliqué shapes on the watermelon blocks.

Note: We suggest pinning a square of tear-away stabilizer to the backside of the blocks so they will lay flat when the machine appliqué is complete.

Step 4 We machine blanket stitched around the shapes using black thread. If you like, you could hand blanket stitch around the shapes with pearl cotton.

blanket stitch

Note: To prevent the hand blanket stitches from "rolling off" the edges of the appliqué shapes, take an extra backstitch in the same place as you made the blanket stitch, going around the outer curves, corners, and points. For straight edges, taking a backstitch every inch is enough.

Border

*Note: The yardage given allows for the border strips to be cut on the crosswise grain. Refer to **Border** instructions on page 121 for general instructions on adding borders.*

Cutting

From **BEIGE** print:
- Cut 7, 2-1/2 x 42-inch border strips.

Attach the 2-1/2-inch wide **BEIGE** border strips to each watermelon block.

Putting It All Together

Trim the backing and batting rectangles so they are 4-inches larger than each of the place mat tops. Refer to **Finishing the Quilt** on page 123 for complete instructions.

Quilting Suggestions:
- Meander the entire place mat.

Binding

Cutting

From **GREEN DIAGONAL PRINT**:

• Cut 7, 2-3/4 x 42-inch strips

Sew the binding to the place mats using a 3/8-inch seam allowance. This measurement will produce a 1/2-inch wide finished double binding. Refer to **Binding** and **Diagonal Piecing** on page 123 for complete instructions.

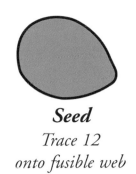

Seed
*Trace 12
onto fusible web*

Melon Patch

Place Mats

12 x 18-inches

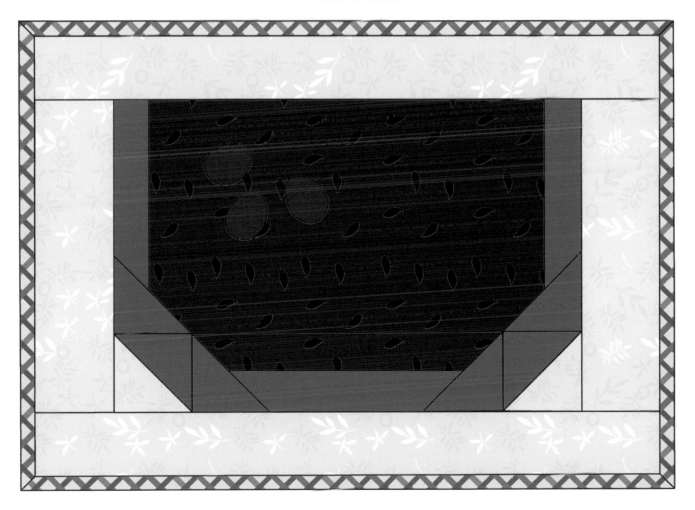

Melon Patch
Napkins

16-inches square

Reversible napkins are always twice as nice, especially when they complement a simple-to-sew tablecloth cut from 108-inch wide fabric that only needs hemming. If it seems like no seams, you're right.

Fabrics and Supplies

1 yard **BLUE FLORAL** for napkins

1 yard **RED PRINT** for napkins

Before beginning this project, read through
General Instructions *on page 110.*

How to Fold the Napkin

Napkin Squares

Cutting

From **BLUE FLORAL:**

- Cut 4, 16-1/2-inch squares

From **RED PRINT:**

- Cut 4, 16-1/2-inch squares

Piecing

Step 1 With right sides together, layer the 16-1/2-inch **BLUE FLORAL** and **RED** squares in pairs. Stitch 1/4-inch from the edges leaving 3-inches open on one side for turning.

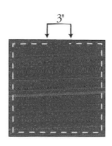

Make 4

Step 2 Clip the corners, turn the napkins right side out; press. Take care to see that the corners are sharp and even.

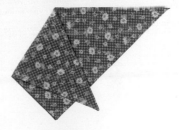

Step 3 Hand stitch the openings closed.

Step 4 Stitch diagonally from corner to corner to stabilize each napkin. Stitch 1/4-inch around the edges.

Make 4

Runner

24 x 38-inches

Flying Geese units create an interesting formation in this restful runner splashed with red and blue for a tabletop salute to summer.

Fabrics and Supplies

2/3 yard **BLUE PRINT**
for flying geese, bands, and outer border

3/8 yard **BEIGE PRINT** for background

3/8 yard **ROSE PRINT**
for inner border and band

1/8 yard **YELLOW PRINT**
for narrow middle border

3/8 yard **YELLOW PRINT** for binding

1-1/4 yards for backing

Quilt batting, at least 30 x 44-inches

*Before beginning this project, read through
General Instructions on page 110.*

Flying Geese Units

Cutting

From **BLUE PRINT**:

- Cut 2 to 3, 2-1/2 x 42-inch strips.
  From the strips cut:
  18, 2-1/2 x 4-1/2-inch rectangles

From **BEIGE PRINT**:

- Cut 3 to 4, 2-1/2 x 42-inch strips.
  From the strips cut:
  18, 2-1/2 x 4-1/2-inch rectangles
  18, 2-1/2-inch squares

Piecing

Step 1   With right sides together, position a 2-1/2 x 4-1/2-inch **BEIGE** rectangle on the left corner of a 2-1/2 x 4-1/2-inch **BLUE** rectangle. Draw a diagonal line on the rectangle and stitch on the line. Trim the seam allowance to 1/4-inch; press. Repeat this process at the right corner of the rectangle using a 2-1/2-inch **BEIGE** square. <u>At this point each flying geese unit should measure 2-1/2 x 6-1/2-inches.</u>

Make 10

Step 2   With right sides together, position a 2-1/2-inch **BEIGE** square on the left corner of a 2-1/2 x 4-1/2-inch **BLUE** rectangle. Draw a diagonal line on the square; stitch, trim, and press. Repeat this process at the right corner of the rectangle using a 2-1/2 x 4-1/2-inch **BEIGE** rectangle. <u>At this point each flying geese unit should measure 2-1/2 x 6-1/2-inches.</u>

Make 8

Step 3 Sew together 5 of the Step 1 units and 4 of the Step 2 units; press. <u>At this point each flying geese section should measure 6-1/2 x 18-1/2-inches.</u>

Make 2

Step 4 Refer to the diagram for placement, and sew together the flying geese sections; press. <u>At this point the runner center should measure 12-1/2 x 18-1/2-inches.</u>

Make 1

Borders

*Note: The yardage given allows for the border strips to be cut on the crosswise grain. Diagonally piece the strips as needed, referring to **Diagonal Piecing** instructions on page 123. Read through **Borders** on page 121 for general instructions on adding borders.*

Cutting

From **ROSE PRINT**:
- Cut 3, 2-1/2 x 42-inch inner border strips
- Cut 1 more 2-1/2 x 42-inch band strip

From **BLUE PRINT**:
- Cut 3, 4 x 42-inch outer border strips
- Cut 1, 2-1/2 x 42-inch band strip

From **YELLOW PRINT**:
- Cut 3, 1 x 42-inch narrow middle border strips

Attaching the Borders

Step 1 Attach the 2-1/2-inch wide **ROSE** inner border strips.

Step 2 Measure the runner from top and bottom through the center to determine the length of the side bands. Cut 2, 2-1/2-inch wide **BLUE** and **ROSE** bands to this length. Sew the bands to the side edges of the runner; press.

Step 3 Attach the 1-inch wide **YELLOW** narrow middle border strips.

Step 4 Attach the 4-inch wide **BLUE** outer border strips.

Putting It All Together

Trim the backing and batting so they are 6-inches larger than the runner top. Refer to **Finishing the Quilt** on page 123 for complete instructions.

Quilting Suggestions:

- **BEIGE** background - stipple.

- **BLUE** flying geese - in-the-ditch.

- **ROSE** inner border - **TB30 Beadwork**.

- **BLUE** outer border - **TB28 Leaf Sketch**.

THIMBLEBERRIES® quilt stencils by Quilting Creations International are available at your local quilt shop.

Binding

Cutting

From **YELLOW PRINT**:
- Cut 4, 2-3/4 x 42-inch strips

Sew the binding to the quilt using a 3/8-inch seam allowance. This measurement will produce a 1/2-inch wide finished double binding. Refer to **Binding** and **Diagonal Piecing** on page 123 for complete instructions.

Summertime

Runner

24 x 38-inches

Picnic Stars

Quilt

54 x 62-inches

Picnic stars pair up with checkerboards for a pleasing patchwork quilt sized right for soaking up the sunshine on a lazy afternoon.

Fabrics and Supplies

2/3 yard **YELLOW PRINT**
for star blocks and first middle border

7/8 yard **BEIGE PRINT**
for star blocks and checkerboard strips

5/8 yard **ROSE PRINT**
for checkerboard strips
and second middle border

3/4 yard **GREEN PRINT**
for lattice strips and inner border

1-5/8 yards **BLUE PRINT**
for outer border

5/8 yard **ROSE PRINT** for binding

3-1/3 yards for backing

Quilt batting, at least 60 x 68-inches

Before beginning this project, read through **General Instructions** *on page 110.*

Star Blocks

Makes 15 blocks

Cutting

From **YELLOW PRINT**:

- Cut 5, 2-1/2 x 42-inch strips. From the strips cut:
  15, 2-1/2 x 6-1/2-inch rectangles
  30, 2-1/2-inch squares

From **BEIGE PRINT**:

- Cut 8, 2-1/2 x 42-inch strips. From the strips cut:
  30, 2-1/2 x 4-1/2-inch rectangles
  60, 2-1/2-inch squares

Piecing

Step 1 With right sides together, position a 2-1/2-inch **YELLOW** square on the right corner of a 2-1/2 x 4-1/2-inch **BEIGE** rectangle. Draw a diagonal line on the square and stitch on the line. Trim the seam allowance to 1/4-inch; press. Sew a 2-1/2-inch **BEIGE** square to right edge of the unit; press. <u>At this point each unit should measure 2-1/2 x 6-1/2-inches.</u>

Make 30

Step 2 With right sides together, position 2-1/2-inch **BEIGE** squares on both corners of a 2-1/2 x 6-1/2-inch **YELLOW** rectangle. Draw a diagonal line on the squares; stitch, trim, and press. <u>At this point each unit should measure 2-1/2 x 6-1/2-inches.</u>

Make 15

Step 3 Sew the Step 1 units to the top/bottom edges of the Step 2 units; press. <u>At this point each star block should measure 6-1/2-inches square.</u>

Make 15

Step 4 Sew 5 of the star blocks together to make a star block strip; press. <u>At this point each star block strip should measure 6-1/2 x 30-1/2-inches.</u>

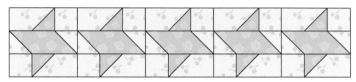

Make 3

Checkerboard Strips

Cutting

From **ROSE PRINT**:

• Cut 3, 2-1/2 x 42-inch strips

From **BEIGE PRINT**:

• Cut 3, 2-1/2 x 42-inch strips

Piecing

Step 1 Aligning long raw edges, sew 2-1/2 x 42-inch **ROSE** strips to both side edges of a 2-1/2 x 42-inch **BEIGE** strip. Press the strip set referring to *Hints and Helps for Pressing Strip Sets*. Cut the strip set into segments.

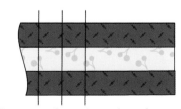

Crosscut 16, 2-1/2-inch wide segments

Hints and Helps for Pressing Strip Sets

When sewing strips of fabric together for strip sets, it is important to press the seam allowances nice and flat, usually to the dark fabric. Be careful not to stretch as you press, causing a "rainbow effect." This will affect the accuracy and shape of the pieces cut from the strip set. Press on the wrong side first with the strips perpendicular to the ironing board. Flip the piece over and press on the right side to prevent little pleats from forming at the seams. Laying the strip set lengthwise on the ironing board seems to encourage the rainbow effect.

Avoid this rainbow effect

Step 2 Aligning long raw edges, sew 2-1/2 x 42-inch **BEIGE** strips to both side edges of a 2-1/2 x 42-inch **ROSE** strip; press. Cut the strip set into segments.

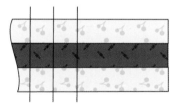

Crosscut 14, 2-1/2-inch wide segments

Step 3 Sew together 8 of the Step 1 segments and 7 of the Step 2 segments; press. <u>At this point each checkerboard strip should measure 6-1/2 x 30-1/2-inches.</u>

Make 2

Quilt Center

Cutting

From **GREEN PRINT**:

- Cut 6, 2-1/2 x 42-inch strips. From the strips cut: 6, 2-1/2 x 30-1/2-inch lattice and top/bottom inner border strips

Quilt Center Assembly

Referring to quilt diagram for block placement, sew together the star block strips, checkerboard strips, and 2-1/2 x 30-1/2-inch **GREEN** lattice and top/bottom inner border strips; press. At this point the quilt center should measure 30-1/2 x 42-1/2-inches.

Borders

*Note: The yardage given allows for the border strips to be cut on the crosswise grain. Diagonally piece the strips as needed, referring to **Diagonal Piecing** instructions on page 123. Read through **Border** instructions on page 121 for general instructions on adding borders.*

Cutting

From **GREEN PRINT**:

- Cut 2, 2-1/2 x 42-inch side inner border strips. You may need to cut 1 extra strip.

From **YELLOW PRINT**:

- Cut 5, 1-1/2 x 42-inch first middle border strips

From **ROSE PRINT**:

- Cut 5, 1-1/2 x 42-inch second middle border strips

From **BLUE PRINT**:

- Cut 6, 8-1/2 x 42-inch outer border strips

Piecing

Step 1 Attach the 2-1/2-inch wide **GREEN** side inner border strips.

Step 2 Attach the 1-1/2-inch wide **YELLOW** first middle border strips.

Step 3 Attach the 1-1/2-inch wide **ROSE** second middle border strips.

Step 4 Attach the 8-1/2-inch wide **BLUE** outer border strips.

Putting It All Together

Cut the 3-1/3 yard length of backing fabric in half crosswise to make 2, 1-2/3 yard lengths. Refer to *Finishing the Quilt* on page 123 for complete instructions.

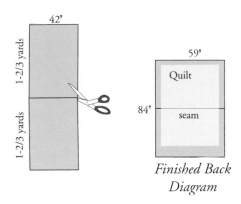

Finished Back Diagram

Quilting Suggestions:

- Star blocks - in-the-ditch and small meander **BEIGE** background.

- **ROSE** checkerboard - large X.

- **BEIGE** checkerboard - small meander.

- **GREEN** lattice and inner border - *Circle of Love*™ small border stencil.

- **YELLOW** and **ROSE** borders - in-the-ditch.

- **BLUE** outer border - *Pansy Park*™ border stencil (fence).

Binding

Cutting

From **ROSE PRINT**:

- Cut 6, 2-3/4 x 42-inch strips

Sew the binding to the quilt using a 3/8-inch seam allowance. This measurement will produce a 1/2-inch wide finished double binding. Refer to *Binding* and *Diagonal Piecing* on page 123 for complete instructions.

Picnic Stars

Quilting Suggestion

Picnic Stars

Quilt

54 x 62-inches

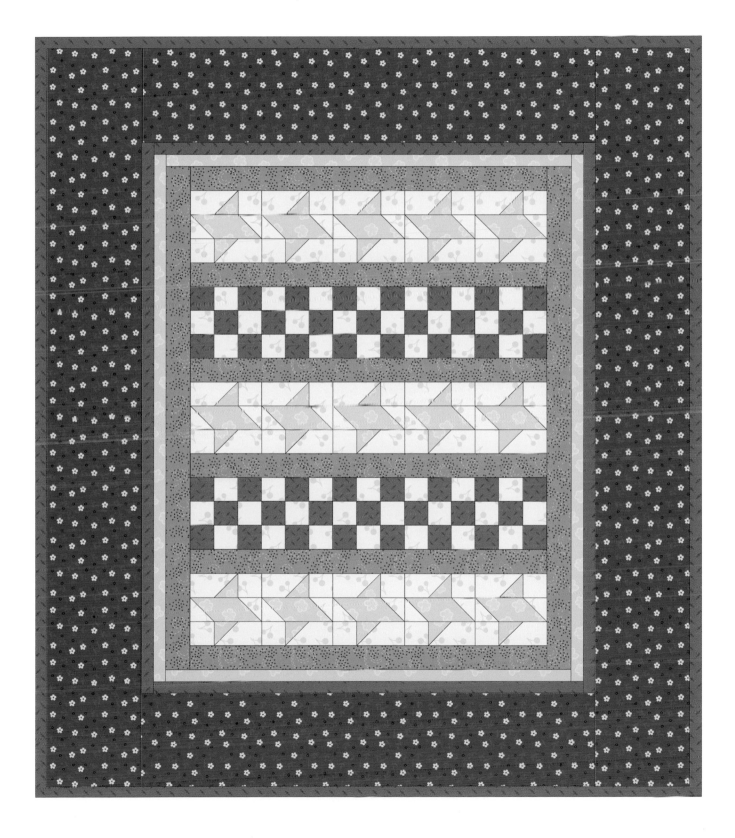

Garden Glory

Quilt

62 x 76-inches

Six pieced blocks make up the center of this stunning Garden Glory Quilt. Sawtooth units, half-post triangles and corner squares make this a floral masterpiece and an afternoon delight.

Fabrics and Supplies

1-1/3 yards **SMALL BLUE FLORAL** for pieced blocks, side and corner triangles, and middle border

5/8 yard **BEIGE PRINT** for sawtooth units

1-1/4 yards **GREEN PRINT** for sawtooth units and inner border

5/8 yard **RED PRINT** for blocks, half-post triangles, and corner squares

2-7/8 yards **LARGE BLUE FLORAL** for alternate blocks and outer border

3/4 yard **RED PLAID** for binding (cut on the bias)

3-3/4 yards for backing fabric

Quilt batting, at least 68 x 82-inches

Before beginning this project, read through **General Instructions** *on page 110.*

Pieced Blocks

Makes 6 blocks

Cutting

From **SMALL BLUE FLORAL**:
- Cut 1, 6-1/2 x 42-inch strip. From the strip cut: 6, 6-1/2-inch squares

From **GREEN PRINT**:
- Cut 6, 2-7/8 x 42-inch strips

From **BEIGE PRINT**:
- Cut 6, 2-7/8 x 42-inch strips

From **RED PRINT**:
- Cut 2, 2-1/2 x 42-inch strips. From the strips cut: 24, 2-1/2-inch squares

Piecing

Step 1 With right sides together, layer the 2-7/8 x 42-inch **GREEN** and **BEIGE** strips together in pairs. Press together, but do not sew. Cut the layered strips into squares. Cut the layered squares in half diagonally to make 144 sets of triangles. Stitch 1/4-inch from the diagonal edge of each pair of triangles; press. <u>At this point each triangle-pieced square should measure 2-1/2-inches square.</u>

Crosscut 72, 2-7/8-inch squares

Make 144, 2-1/2-inch triangle-pieced squares

Step 2 Referring to the diagrams, sew the triangle-pieced squares together in sets of 3; press. <u>At this point each sawtooth unit should measure 2-1/2 x 6-1/2-inches.</u>

Make 24　　*Make 24*
Unit A　　*Unit B*

Step 3 Sew **A** sawtooth units to the top/bottom edges of each 6-1/2-inch **SMALL BLUE FLORAL** square; press. Sew 2-1/2-inch **RED** squares to both ends of 12 of the **B** sawtooth units; press. Sew the units to the side edges of the **SMALL BLUE FLORAL** square; press. <u>At this point each pieced block should measure 10-1/2-inches square.</u>

Note: Set the remaining sawtooth units aside to be used in the side/corner triangles.

 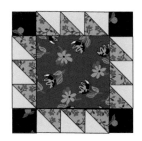

Make 6

Quilt Center

Note: The side, corner, and half-post triangles are larger than necessary and will be trimmed before the borders are added.

Cutting

From **LARGE BLUE FLORAL**:
- Cut 4, 10-1/2 x 42-inch strips. From the strips cut: 12, 10-1/2-inch alternate blocks

From **SMALL BLUE FLORAL**:
- Cut 1, 10-1/2 x 42-inch strip. From the strip cut: 3, 10-1/2-inch squares. Cut the squares diagonally into quarters for a total of 12 triangles. You will be using only 10 for side triangles.
- Cut 1, 6 x 42-inch strip. From the strip cut: 2, 6-inch squares. Cut the squares in half diagonally to make 4 corner triangles.

From **RED PRINT**:
- Cut 1, 4-1/2 x 42-inch strip. From the strip cut: 7, 4-1/2-inch squares. Cut the squares diagonally into quarters to make 28 half-post triangles.
- Cut 1, 2-1/2 x 42-inch strip. From the strip cut: 10, 2-1/2-inch squares

Quilt Center Assembly

Step 1 Referring to the diagrams, sew a **RED** half-post triangle to the left edge of 6 of the **A** sawtooth units; press. Sew the units to the top edge of 6 of the **SMALL BLUE FLORAL** side triangles; press.

Make 6

Make 6

Step 2 Referring to the diagram, sew a **RED** half-post triangle to the right edge of 6 of the **B** sawtooth units; press. Sew a 2-1/2-inch **RED** square to the left edge of the units; press. Sew the units to the right edge of the Step 1 units to make 6 pieced side triangles which will be used for the **side edges** of the quilt. The side and half-post triangles are larger than necessary and will be trimmed before the borders are added.

Make 6

*Make 6
pieced side
triangles*

Step 3 Referring to the diagrams, sew a **RED** half-post triangle to the left edge of 4 of the **B** sawtooth units; press. Sew the units to the top edge of 4 of the **SMALL BLUE FLORAL** side triangles; press.

Make 4

Make 4

Step 4 Referring to the diagrams, sew a **RED** half-post triangle to the right edge of 4 of the **A** sawtooth units; press. Sew a 2-1/2-inch **RED** square to the left edge of the units; press. Sew the units to the right edge of the Step 3 units to make 4 side triangles which will be used for the **top/bottom edges** of the quilt.

Make 4

Make 4 pieced side triangles

Step 5 Referring to the quilt assembly diagram on page 68, sew together the pieced blocks, alternate blocks, and side triangles in 6 diagonal rows. Press the seam allowances toward the alternate blocks. Pin the block rows together; sew and press.

Step 6 Sew **RED** half-post triangles to both side edges of 2 of the **A** sawtooth units; press. Sew the units to the top edge of 2 of the **SMALL BLUE FLORAL** corner triangles to make 2 pieced corner triangles.

Make 2

Make 2 pieced corner triangles

Repeat this process using the **B** sawtooth units to make 2 pieced corner triangles. Sew the pieced corner triangles to the quilt center; press.

Make 2

Make 2 pieced corner triangles

Step 7 Trim away the excess fabric from the side, corner, and half-post triangles taking care to allow a 1/4-inch seam allowance beyond the corners of each block. Refer to *Trimming Side and Corner Triangles* for complete instructions.

Trimming Side and Corner Triangles

Begin at a corner by lining up your ruler 1/4-inch beyond the points of the block corners as shown. Cut along the edge of the ruler. Repeat this procedure on all four sides of the quilt top.

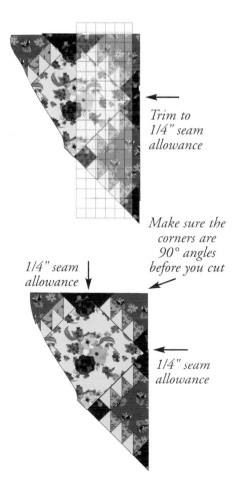
Trim to 1/4" seam allowance

Make sure the corners are 90° angles before you cut

1/4" seam allowance

1/4" seam allowance

Quilt Assembly Diagram

Borders

Note: *The yardage given allows for the border strips to be cut on the crosswise grain. Diagonally piece the strips as needed, referring to* **Diagonal Piecing** *instructions on page 123. Read through* **Border** *instructions on page 121 for general instructions on adding borders.*

Cutting

From **GREEN PRINT**:
  • Cut 7, 2-1/2 x 42-inch inner border strips

From **SMALL BLUE FLORAL**:
  • Cut 7, 2-1/2 x 42-inch middle border strips

From **RED PRINT**:
  • Cut 4, 4-1/2-inch corner squares

From **LARGE BLUE FLORAL**:
  • Cut 8, 6-1/2 x 42-inch outer border strips

Attaching the Borders

Step 1 For the top/bottom inner and middle borders, measure the quilt from left to right through the middle. Cut 2, 2-1/2-inch wide **GREEN** inner border strips to this length and cut 2, 2-1/2-inch wide **SMALL BLUE FLORAL** middle border strips to this length.

Step 2 Aligning long edges, sew together the 2-1/2-inch wide **GREEN** and **SMALL BLUE FLORAL** strips in pairs; press. Sew the pieced border strips to the top/bottom edges of the quilt center; press.

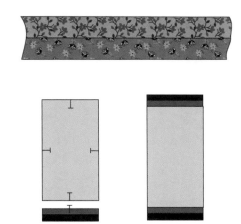

Step 3 For the side inner and middle borders, measure the quilt from top to bottom including the seam allowances, but not the top/bottom borders just added. Cut the 2, 2-1/2-inch wide **GREEN** inner border strips to this length and cut 2, 2-1/2-inch wide **SMALL BLUE FLORAL** middle border strips to this length.

Step 4 Aligning long edges, sew together the 2-1/2-inch wide **GREEN** and **SMALL BLUE FLORAL** strips in pairs; press. Sew the 4-1/2-inch **RED** corner square to both ends of the pieced border strips; press. Sew the pieced border strips to the side edges of the quilt center; press.

Step 5 Attach the 6-1/2-inch wide **LARGE BLUE FLORAL** outer border strips.

Putting It All Together

Cut the 3-3/4 yard length of backing fabric in half crosswise to make 2, 1-7/8 yard lengths. Refer to *Finishing the Quilt* on page 123 for complete instructions.

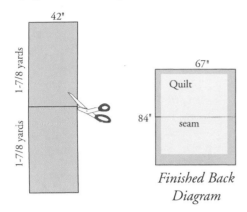

Finished Back Diagram

Quilting Suggestions:

- **LARGE BLUE FLORAL** alternate blocks - **TB24 Floral Burst.**

- Pieced blocks - **TB7 Leaf Quarter.**

- Side triangles - 1/2 of **TB7 Leaf Quarter.**

- Corner triangles - 1/4 of **TB7 Leaf Quarter.**

- **GREEN** and **SMALL BLUE FLORAL** borders - quilt as one border **TB48 Border Heart.**

- **RED** corner squares - **TB24 Floral Burst** (center flower only)

- **LARGE BLUE FLORAL** outer border - **TB36 Flutter Bug.**

THIMBLEBERRIES® *quilt stencils by Quilting Creations International are available at your local quilt shop.*

Binding

Cutting

From **RED PLAID**:

- Cut enough 2-3/4-inch wide *bias* strips to make a 290-inch long strip.

Sew the binding to the quilt using a 3/8-inch seam allowance. This measurement will produce a 1/2-inch wide finished double binding. Refer to *Binding* and *Diagonal Piecing* on page 123 for complete instructions.

Garden Glory

Quilting Suggestion

Garden Glory

Quilt

62 x 76-inches

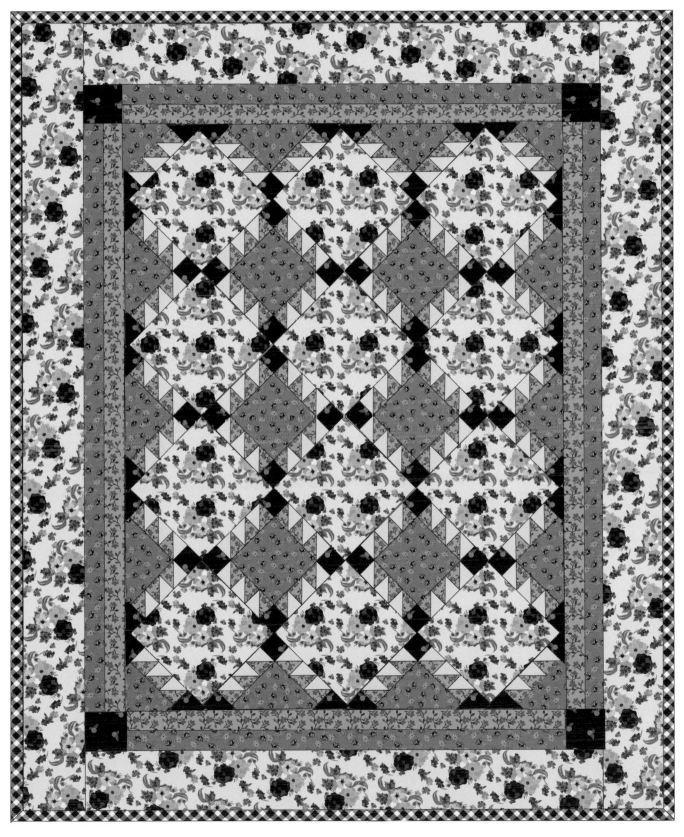

Evening Glow

As dusk approaches, the lingering evening shadows are softened with the warmth and comfort of quilts and harvest-themed table toppers. Outdoors, celebrate by candlelight with a Chevron Log Cabin patchwork quilt for the harvest table. Indoors, a classic Paddlewheel Surround quilt offers a natural centerpiece for the dining table. Or, finish off your day in the evening glow with quick-to-make table toppers like the Autumn Runner or Harvest Table Square.

Runner

24 x 42-inches

Add drama to your dinner table with an autumn runner featuring an oval center. A curved edge template (on page 78) offers quick cutting for the center oval and triangle-pieced squares make up the sawtooth border.

Fabrics and Supplies

1/2 yard **LARGE RED FLORAL**
for center oval

2/3 yard **GOLD/RED PRINT**
for inner border

1 yard **BLACK/BROWN PRINT**
for sawtooth border, binding
for center oval (cut on the bias),
and binding for outside edge

1/3 yard **GREEN PRINT**
for triangle-pieced squares

1-1/3 yards for backing

Quilt batting, at least 30 x 48-inches

Before beginning this project, read through
General Instructions *on page 110.*

Table Runner Center

Cutting

From **LARGE RED FLORAL**:

- Cut 1, 13-1/2 x 31-inch rectangle

From **GOLD/RED PRINT**:

- Cut 1, 18-1/2 x 36-1/2-inch rectangle

From **BLACK/BROWN PRINT**:

- Cut 2, 3-7/8 x 42-inch strips - set the strips aside to be used in the sawtooth border
- Cut enough 2-inch wide **bias** strips to make a strip 85-inches long

Piecing

Step 1 To mark the curved edges on the 13-1/2 x 31-inch **LARGE RED FLORAL** rectangle, use the curved edge template on page 78. Position the template on one narrow end of the rectangle, having all edges even. Cut along the curve of the template as shown. Repeat for the opposite end of the rectangle. Cut the long edges even with the 2 curved edges as shown.

Step 2 With right sides facing up, center the **LARGE RED FLORAL** oval on the 18-1/2 x 36-1/2-inch **GOLD/RED** rectangle. Measure all the sides to be certain the oval is centered; hand baste in place.

*Note: We suggest <u>not</u> cutting away the **GOLD/RED** fabric behind the **LARGE RED FLORAL** oval. This double thickness will give your table runner more stability.*

Step 3 Diagonally piece the 2-inch wide **BLACK/BROWN** bias strips to make a strip 85-inches long. Fold the strip in half lengthwise, wrong sides together; press. Unfold and trim one end at a 45-degree angle. Turn under the edge 1/4-inch; press. Refold the strip.

Diagonal Piecing

Stitch diagonally   Trim to 1/4" seam allowance   Press seam open

Double-Layer Binding

Fold Line

Step 4 Lay the prepared binding strip on the **LARGE RED FLORAL** oval, aligning raw edges.

Align raw edges
Binding Strip

Note: As you stitch, gently ease a little extra binding onto the curved edges. This will prevent the curved edges from "cupping" when finished. "Cupping" happens when you stretch the binding as it is being stitched on.

Step 5 Stitch through all the layers with a 1/4-inch seam allowance. Trim the end of the binding so it can be tucked inside of the beginning binding about 3/8-inch. Finish stitching the seam.

Step 6 Fold the binding strip over onto the **GOLD/RED** inner border so the raw edges are covered. Hand stitch in place along the folded edge with matching thread.

Sawtooth Border

Cutting

From **GREEN PRINT**:

- Cut 2, 3-7/8 x 42-inch strips

The 2 **BLACK/BROWN PRINT** 3-7/8 x 42-inch strips were cut previously.

Piecing

Step 1 With right sides together, layer the 3-7/8 x 42-inch **GREEN** and **BLACK/BROWN** strips in pairs. Press together, but do not sew. Cut the layered strips into squares. Cut the layered squares in half diagonally to make 40 sets of triangles. Stitch 1/4-inch from the diagonal edge of each pair of triangles; press.

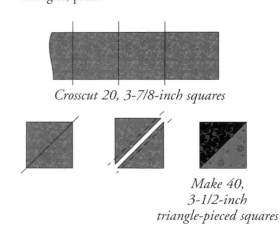

Crosscut 20, 3-7/8-inch squares

Make 40, 3-1/2-inch triangle-pieced squares

Step 2 To make the sawtooth borders for the short ends of the runner, sew together 6 triangle-pieced squares; press. (Notice the direction of the angles). Sew the sawtooth borders to the short ends of the runner; press.

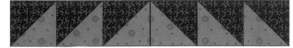

Make 2

Step 3 To make the sawtooth borders for the long ends of the runner, sew together 14 triangle-pieced squares; press. (Notice the direction of the angles). Sew the sawtooth borders to the long ends of the runner; press.

Make 2

Putting It All Together

Trim the backing and batting so they are 6-inches larger than the runner top. Refer to **Finishing the Quilt** on page 123 for complete instructions.

Quilting Suggestions:

• **LARGE RED FLORAL** center oval and **GOLD/RED** inner border - medium meander.

• Sawtooth border - echo and in-the-ditch.

Binding

Cutting

From **BLACK/BROWN PRINT**:

• Cut 4, 2-1/2 x 42-inch strips.
  To maintain perfect triangle tips at the outer edges, sew the binding to the quilt using a 1/4-inch seam allowance. This measurement will produce a 3/8-inch wide finished double binding. Refer to **Binding** and **Diagonal Piecing** on page 123 for complete instructions.

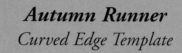

Autumn Runner
Curved Edge Template

Place on fold

Autumn

Runner

24 x 42-inches

Square

40-inches square

A bouquet of autumn's finest gatherings from the garden complement a Harvest Table Square in pumpkin and black fabric prints. The quilt center and pieced border work up quickly into a 40-inch square for a table topper that comes in handy for an impromptu soup supper individually served up piping hot in plaid thermos bottles.

Fabrics and Supplies

3/4 yard **PUMPKIN PRINT**
for center square and corner squares

2-1/2 x 20-inch pieces of
12 ASSORTED BLACK PRINTS
for pieced border

5/8 yard **GREEN FLORAL**
for outer border

1/2 yard **PUMPKIN STRIPE**
for binding

2-1/2 yards for backing

Note: *If your backing fabric is 45-inches wide you will need only 1-1/4 yards for backing.*

Quilt batting, at least 45-inches square

Before beginning this project, read through ***General Instructions*** *on page 110.*

Quilt Center and Pieced Border

Cutting

From **PUMPKIN PRINT**:

- Cut 1, 24-1/2-inch center square
- Cut 4, 4-1/2-inch corner squares

From **12 ASSORTED BLACK PRINTS**:

- Cut 48, 2-1/2 x 4-1/2-inch rectangles

Piecing

Step 1 With right sides together, sew together 12 of the 2-1/2 x 4-1/2-inch **ASSORTED BLACK** rectangles; press. Make 4 pieced borders. At this point each pieced border should measure 4-1/2 x 24-1/2-inches.

Make 4

Step 2 Sew pieced borders to the top/bottom edges of the 24-1/2-inch **PUMPKIN** center square; press. Sew 4-1/2-inch **PUMPKIN** corner squares to both ends of the remaining pieced borders; press. Sew the pieced borders to the side edges of the quilt center; press. At this point the quilt center should measure 32-1/2-inches square.

Borders

*Note: The yardage given allows for the border strips to be cut on the crosswise grain. Read through **Border** instructions on page 121 for general instructions on adding borders.*

Cutting

From **GREEN FLORAL**:

- Cut 4, 4-1/2 x 42-inch outer border strips

Attach the 4-1/2-inch wide **GREEN FLORAL** outer border strips.

Putting It All Together

Cut the 2-1/2 yard length of backing fabric in half crosswise to make 2, 1-1/4 yard lengths. Refer to *Finishing the Quilt* on page 123 for complete instructions.

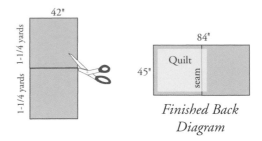

Finished Back Diagram

Quilting Suggestions:

- Center square - **TB11 Pumpkin Flurry** with crosshatching in the background.

- Pieced border and outer border, quilt as one - **TB26 Acorn Vine Border**.

THIMBLEBERRIES® quilt stencils by Quilting Creations International are available at your local quilt shop.

Binding

Cutting

From **PUMPKIN STRIPE**:

- Cut 4, 2-3/4 x 42-inch strips

Sew the binding to the quilt using a 3/8-inch seam allowance. This measurement will produce a 1/2-inch wide finished double binding. Refer to *Binding* and *Diagonal Piecing* on page 123 for complete instructions.

Harvest Table
Square

40-inches square

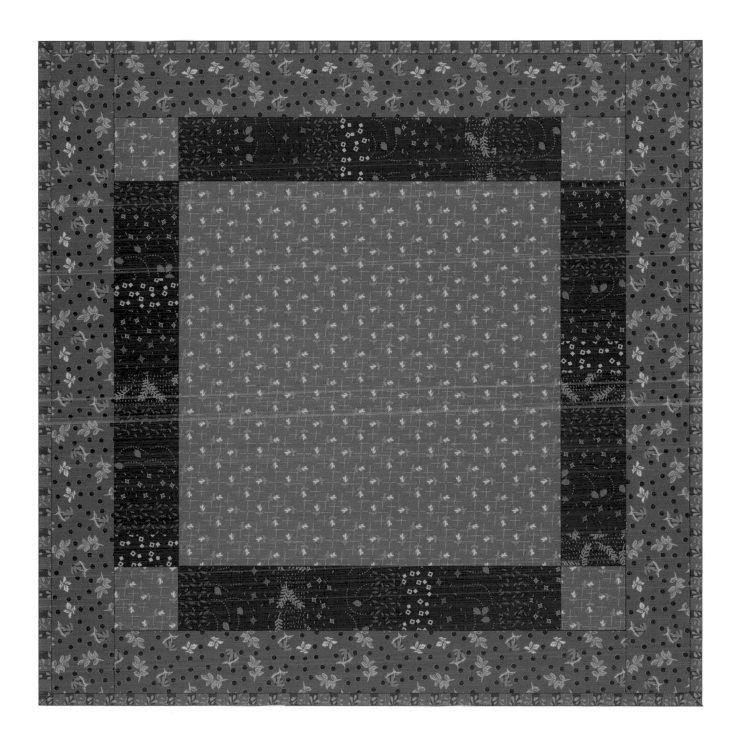

Fabrics and Supplies

1-1/8 yards **EGGPLANT PRINT**
for pinwheel blocks
and large leaf appliqués

3/8 yard **BEIGE PRINT**
for pinwheel blocks

7/8 yard **GREEN PRINT**
for pinwheel blocks and
second middle border

2-1/2 yards **LARGE TAN FLORAL**
for quilt center, inner border,
and outer border

1 yard **GOLD/RED PRINT**
for side/corner triangles, and
first middle border

3/8 yard **GOLD PRINT**
for small leaf and inner circle appliqués

8-inch square **BLACK PRINT**
for outer circle appliqué

2/3 yard **GREEN PRINT** for binding

4 yards for backing

Quilt batting, at least 72-inches square

Paper-backed fusible web

Machine embroidery thread or
pearl cotton for decorative stitches: black

Template material

Tear-away fabric stabilizer

*Before beginning this project, read through
General Instructions on page 110.*

Paddlewheel Surround

Quilt

65-inches square

*Piece together a dozen pinwheel
blocks and appliqué a circle
of oak leaves to the center for a
unique Paddlewheel Surround
Quilt that offers a natural
centerpiece for the harvest table.*

Pinwheel Blocks

Makes 12 blocks

Cutting

From **EGGPLANT PRINT**:
- Cut 2, 5-1/4 x 42-inch strips. From the strips cut:
  12, 5-1/4-inch squares. Cut the squares
  diagonally into quarters to make 48 triangles.

From **BEIGE PRINT**:
- Cut 2, 5-1/4 x 42-inch strips. From the strips cut:
  12, 5-1/4-inch squares. Cut the squares
  diagonally into quarters to make 48 triangles.

From **GREEN PRINT**:
- Cut 3, 4-7/8 x 42-inch strips. From the strips cut: 24, 4-7/8-inch squares. Cut the squares in half diagonally to make 48 triangles.

Piecing

Step 1 With right sides together, layer an **EGGPLANT** triangle on a **BEIGE** triangle. Stitch along one bias edge; press. Repeat this process to make 48 sets of triangles, stitching along the same bias edge of each triangle set.

Bias edges

Make 48

Step 2 Sew a **GREEN** triangle to each of the Step 1 triangle sets; press. <u>At this point each pieced square should measure 4-1/2-inches square.</u>

Make 48

Step 3 Sew the Step 2 pieced squares together in pairs; press. Sew the pairs together to make a pinwheel block; press. <u>At this point each pinwheel block should measure 8-1/2-inches square.</u>

Make 24

Make 12

Fusible Web Appliqué Method

Cutting

From **LARGE TAN FLORAL**:
- Cut 1, 24-1/2-inch center square

Prepare the Appliqués

Step 1 Make templates using the shapes on pages 89-91. Trace the shapes on the paper side of the fusible web, leaving a small margin between each shape. Cut the shapes apart.

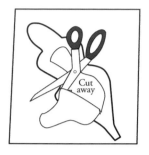 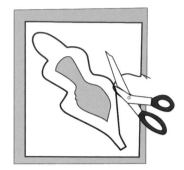

Note: When you are fusing a large shape like the leaf, fuse just the outer edges of the shape so that it will not look stiff when finished. To do this, draw a line about 3/8-inch inside the leaf and cut away the fusible web on this line.

Step 2 Following the manufacturer's instructions, fuse the shapes to the wrong side of the fabric chosen for the appliqués. Let the fabric cool and cut along the traced line. Peel away the paper backing from the fusible web.

Step 3 Referring to the photograph, position the appliqué shapes on the **LARGE TAN FLORAL** 24-1/2-inch center square.

Note: We suggest pinning a square of tear-away stabilizer to the backside of the center square so it will lay flat when the machine appliqué is complete.

Step 4 We machine blanket stitched around the shapes using black thread. You could hand blanket stitch around the shapes with pearl cotton.

blanket stitch

Note: To prevent the hand blanket stitches from "rolling off" the edges of the appliqué shapes, take an extra backstitch in the same place as you made the blanket stitch, going around the outer curves, corners, and points. For straight edges, taking a backstitch every inch is enough.

Quilt Center

Note: The side and corner triangles are larger than necessary and will be trimmed before the borders are added.

Cutting

From **LARGE TAN FLORAL**:
- Cut 1, 8-1/2 x 42-inch strip. From the strip cut:
  4, 8-1/2-inch squares

From **GOLD/RED PRINT**:
- Cut 1, 13 x 42-inch strip. From the strip cut:
  3, 13-inch squares. Cut the squares diagonally into quarters to make 12 side triangles.

Side triangles

- Cut 1, 8 x 42-inch strip. From the strip cut:
  2, 8-inch squares. Cut the squares in half diagonally to make 4 corner triangles.

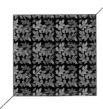

Corner triangles

Quilt Center Assembly

Step 1 Referring to the diagram for placement, sew together 3 of the pinwheel blocks, 1 of the 8-1/2-inch **LARGE TAN FLORAL** squares, and 2 of the side triangles in 2 rows. Press the seam allowances toward the **LARGE TAN FLORAL** block and side triangles. Sew the rows together; press. Make 2 corner units. Sew the corner units to the side edges of the 24-1/2-inch **LARGE TAN FLORAL** center square; press.

Make 2 corner units

Step 2 Referring to the diagram for placement, sew together 3 of the pinwheel blocks, 1 of the 8-1/2-inch **LARGE TAN FLORAL** squares, and 4 of the side triangles in 2 rows. Press the seam allowances toward the **LARGE TAN FLORAL** block and side triangles. Sew the rows together; press. Make 2 corner units. Referring to the quilt diagram, sew the corner units to the side edges of the center square unit; press.

Make 2 corner units

Step 3 Sew the **GOLD/RED PRINT** corner triangles to the quilt center; press.

Step 4 Trim away the excess fabric from the side and corner triangles taking care to allow a 1/4-inch seam allowance beyond the corners of each block. Read through *Trimming Side and Corner Triangles* on page 116 for complete instructions. At this point the quilt center should measure 45-1/2-inches square.

Borders

*Note: The yardage given allows for the border strips to be cut on the crosswise grain. Diagonally piece the strips as needed, referring to **Diagonal Piecing** instructions on page 123. Read through **Border** instructions on page 121 for general instructions on adding borders.*

Cutting

From **LARGE TAN FLORAL**:
- Cut 13, 4-1/2 x 42-inch inner border and outer border strips

From **GOLD/RED PRINT**:
- Cut 6, 1-1/2 x 42-inch first middle border strips

From **GREEN PRINT**:
- Cut 6, 1-1/2 x 42-inch second middle border strips

Attaching the Borders

Step 1 Attach the 4-1/2-inch wide **LARGE TAN FLORAL** inner border strips.

Step 2 Attach the 1-1/2-inch wide **GOLD/RED PRINT** first middle border strips.

Step 3 Attach the 1-1/2-inch wide **GREEN PRINT** second middle border strips.

Step 4 Attach the 4-1/2-inch wide **LARGE TAN FLORAL** outer border strips.

Putting It All Together

Cut the 4 yard length of backing fabric in half crosswise to make 2, 2 yard lengths. Refer to *Finishing the Quilt* on page 123 for complete instructions.

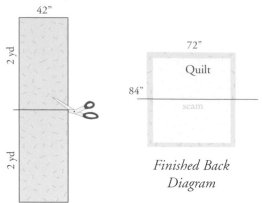

Finished Back Diagram

Quilting Suggestions:

- Inner border - **TB31 Blossom Swirl**.

- 4 **LARGE TAN FLORAL** 8-1/2-inch quilt center squares – **TB13 Bur Oak**.

THIMBLEBERRIES® *quilt stencils by Quilting Creations International are available at your local quilt shop.*

Binding

Cutting

From **GREEN PRINT**:
- Cut 7, 2-3/4 x 42-inch strips

Sew the binding to the quilt using a 3/8-inch seam allowance. This measurement will produce a 1/2-inch wide finished double binding. Refer to *Binding* and *Diagonal Piecing* on page 123 for complete instructions.

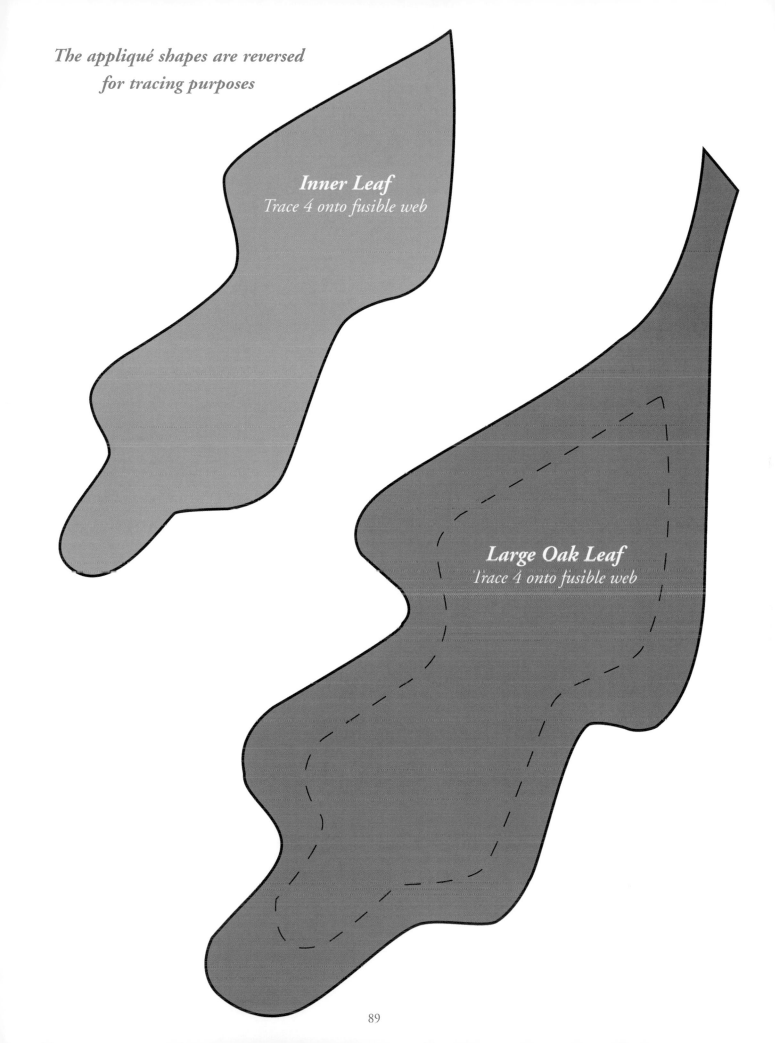

The appliqué shapes are reversed for tracing purposes

Inner Leaf
Trace 4 onto fusible web

Large Oak Leaf
Trace 4 onto fusible web

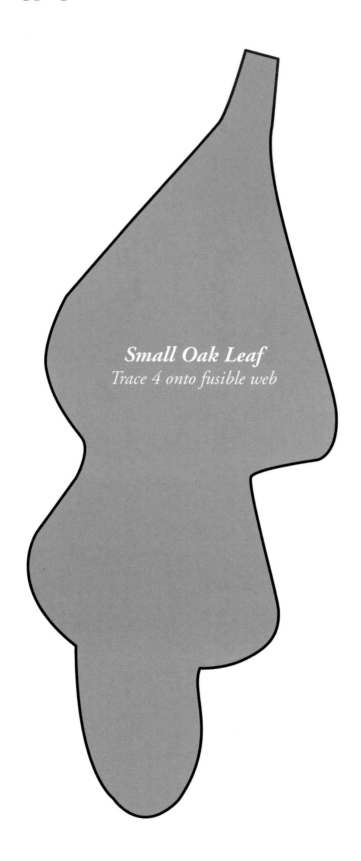

Small Oak Leaf
Trace 4 onto fusible web

The appliqué shapes are reversed
for tracing purposes

Small Center Circle
Trace 1 onto fusible web

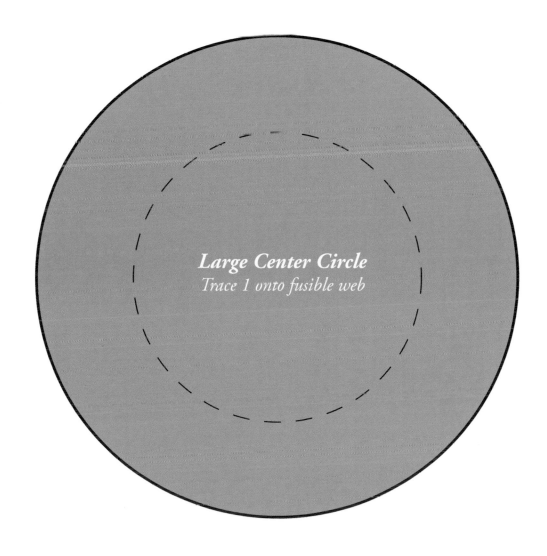

Large Center Circle
Trace 1 onto fusible web

Paddlewheel Surround

Quilting Suggestion

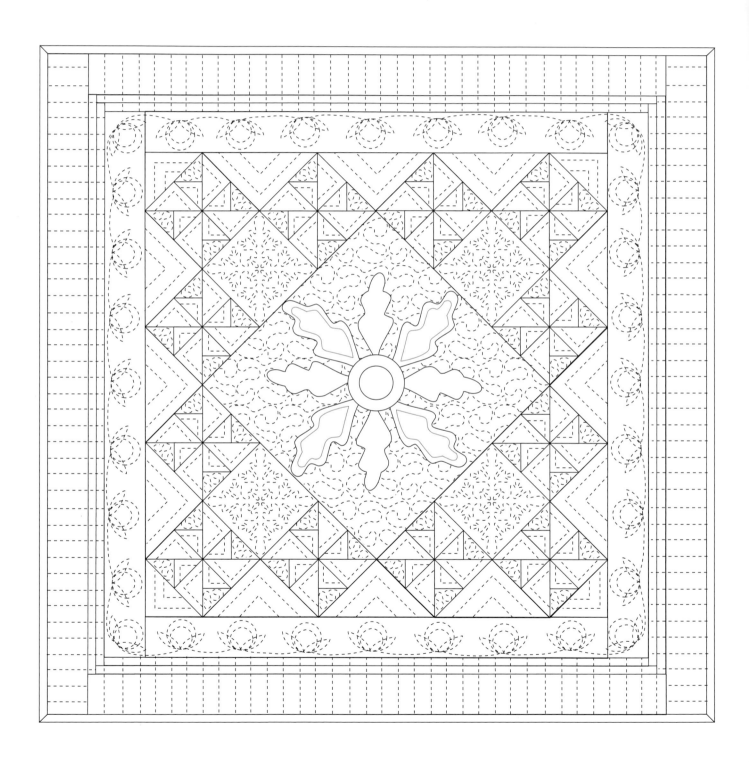

Paddlewheel Surround

Quilt

65-inches square

Fabrics and Supplies

5/8 yard **BARN RED PRINT**
for house, inner border, and berry appliqués

5 x 20-inch piece **COCOA PRINT**
for windows

1-1/4 yards **BLACK PRINT**
for house, quilt center, pumpkin units,
and picket fence border

6 x 42-inch piece **ORANGE PRINT**
for star points

1-1/3 yards **DARK GREEN PRINT**
for house, vine appliqués, pumpkin stems,
and outer border

1/4 yard **ORANGE PUMPKIN PRINT**
for star center and outer pumpkin units

1/8 yard **ORANGE FLORAL**
for star center and inner pumpkin units

2/3 yard **TAN FLORAL**
for picket fence border

1/8 yard **MEDIUM GREEN PRINT**
for leaf appliqués

5/8 yard **BARN RED PRINT** for binding

3 yards for backing

Quilt batting, at least 52 x 59-inches

Paper-backed fusible web

Machine embroidery thread or pearl cotton
for decorative stitches: black

Template material

Tear-away fabric stabilizer

*Before beginning this project,
read through **General Instructions** on page 110.*

Pumpkin House

Wall Quilt

46 x 53-inches

*Bring the best of the garden indoors
with a Pumpkin House Wall Quilt—
complete with a picket fence. From
the appliquéd windows to the star
in the sky, this charming scene simply
glows with warmth and welcome.*

Quilt Center

Cutting

From **BARN RED PRINT:**
- Cut 1, 3-1/2 x 42-inch strip. From the strip cut:
  - 2, 3-1/2-inch squares
  - 2, 2-1/2 x 7-7/8-inch rectangles
  - 2, 2-1/2 x 3-1/2-inch rectangles
- Cut 1, 2 x 42-inch strip. From the strip cut:
  - 2, 2 x 10-1/2-inch rectangles
- Cut 2, 1-1/2 x 42-inch strips. From the strips cut:
  - 2, 1-1/2 x 10-1/2-inch rectangles
  - 6, 1-1/2 x 3-1/2-inch rectangles
  - 12, 1-1/2-inch squares

From **COCOA PRINT:**
- Cut 1, 3-1/2 x 20-inch strip. From the strip cut:
  - 5, 3-1/2-inch squares
  - 1, 1-1/2 x 2-1/2-inch rectangle

From **BLACK PRINT:**

- Cut 2, 5-1/2 x 42-inch strips. From the strips cut:
  2, 5-1/2 x 26-1/2-inch appliqué
  foundation rectangles
  2, 1-1/2 x 24-1/2-inch border strips
  (diagonally piece the strips as needed)
- Cut 1, 3-1/2 x 42-inch strip. From the strip cut:
  3, 3-1/2 x 6-1/2-inch rectangles
  2, 3-1/2 x 5-1/2-inch rectangles
  2, 3-1/2-inch squares
- Cut 1, 2-1/2 x 42-inch strip. From the strip cut:
  2, 2-1/2 x 7-7/8-inch rectangles
  2, 1-1/2 x 9-1/2-inch rectangles
- Cut 2, 1-1/2 x 42-inch strips. From the strips cut:
  2, 1-1/2 x 5-1/2-inch rectangles
  1, 1-1/2 x 2-1/2-inch rectangle
  21, 1-1/2-inch squares

From **ORANGE PRINT:**

- Cut 1, 3-7/8 x 42-inch strip. From the strip cut:
  2, 3-7/8 x 7-7/8-inch rectangles
  6, 3-1/2-inch squares

From **DARK GREEN PRINT:**

- Cut 1, 7-7/8 x 42-inch strip. From the strip cut:
  2, 7-7/8-inch squares
  1, 3-1/2 x 14-1/2-inch rectangle
  2, 3-1/2-inch squares
  8, 1-1/2-inch squares

From **ORANGE PUMPKIN PRINT:**

- Cut 3, 2-1/2 x 42-inch strips. From the strips cut:
  10, 2-1/2 x 6-1/2-inch rectangles
  12, 1-1/2-inch squares

From **ORANGE FLORAL:**

- Cut 1, 2-1/2 x 42-inch strip. From the strip cut:
  5, 2-1/2 x 6-1/2-inch rectangles

Quilt Center Assembly

Step 1 To make the window units, with right sides together, position 2 of the 1-1/2-inch **BARN RED** squares on the upper corners of a 3-1/2-inch **COCOA**

square. Draw a diagonal line on the **BARN RED** squares and stitch on the lines. Trim the seam allowances to 1/4-inch; press.

Make 5 window units

Step 2 To make the door unit, sew together a 1-1/2-inch **BLACK** square, a 1-1/2 x 2-1/2-inch **COCOA** rectangle, and a 1-1/2 x 2-1/2-inch **BLACK** rectangle; press. Sew 1-1/2 x 5-1/2-inch **BLACK** rectangles to the side edges of the unit; press. With right sides together, position 2 of the 1-1/2-inch **BARN RED** squares on the upper corners of the unit. Draw a diagonal line on the squares; stitch, trim, and press. At this point the door unit should measure 3-1/2 x 5-1/2-inches.

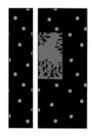

Make 1 door unit

Step 3 Sew together 2 of the window units, 2 of the 1-1/2 x 3-1/2-inch **BARN RED** rectangles, and 1 of the 2-1/2 x 3-1/2-inch **BARN RED** rectangles; press. At this point each window unit should measure 3-1/2 x 10-1/2-inches.

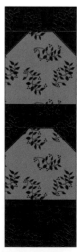

Make 2 window units

Step 4 Sew together 1 of the window units, 2 of the 1-1/2 x 3-1/2-inch **BARN RED** rectangles, and the door unit; press. At this point the door/window unit should measure 3-1/2 x 10-1/2-inches.

Make 1 door/window unit

Step 5 Referring to the diagram, sew together the window units, the door/window unit, and the 1-1/2 x 10-1/2-inch **BARN RED** rectangles; press. Sew the 2 x 10-1/2-inch **BARN RED** rectangles to the side edges of the unit; press. At this point the house base should measure 10-1/2 x 14-1/2-inches.

Step 6 To prepare the roof unit, aligning long edges, sew together a 2-1/2 x 7-7/8-inch **BARN RED** rectangle, a 2-1/2 x 7-7/8-inch **BLACK** rectangle, and a 3-7/8 x 7-7/8-inch **ORANGE PRINT** rectangle; press. Make 2 units. At this point each unit should measure 7-7/8-inches square.

Make 2

Step 7 To make the left roof top unit, refer to the diagrams. Position a 7-7/8-inch **DARK GREEN** square on a Step 6 unit (be sure to have the **ORANGE PRINT** strip on the right hand side). Cut the layered squares diagonally in half (notice the direction of the cutting line). Stitch 1/4-inch from the diagonal edge; press. Position a 3-1/2-inch **BARN RED** square on the lower right corner of the pieced square. Draw a diagonal line on the **BARN RED** square; stitch, trim, and press. At this point the left roof top unit should measure 7-1/2-inches square.

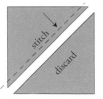

Make 1 left roof top unit

Step 8 To make the right roof top unit, refer to the diagrams. Position a 7-7/8-inch **DARK GREEN** square on a Step 6 unit (be sure to have the **ORANGE PRINT** strip on the left hand side). Cut the layered squares diagonally in half (notice the direction of the cutting line). Stitch 1/4-inch from the diagonal edge; press. Position a 3-1/2-inch **BARN RED** square on the lower left corner of the pieced square. Draw a diagonal line on the **BARN RED** square; stitch, trim, and press. At this point the right roof top unit should measure 7-1/2-inches square.

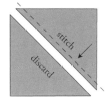

Make 1 right roof top unit

Step 9 Sew together the 2 roof top units; press. Referring to the quilt diagram, sew the roof unit to the house base unit; press. At this point the quilt center should measure 14-1/2 x 17-1/2-inches.

Make 1 roof top unit

Step 10 To make the star center unit, with right sides together, position 1-1/2-inch **ORANGE PUMPKIN PRINT** squares on 2 opposite corners of a 2-1/2 x 6-1/2-inch **ORANGE FLORAL** rectangle. Draw a diagonal line on the squares; stitch, trim, and press. Repeat this process at the remaining corners of the rectangle. Make 1 unit.

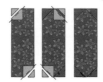

Make 1

Sew 2-1/2 x 6-1/2-inch **ORANGE PUMPKIN PRINT** rectangles to both side edges of the unit; press. With right sides together, position 1-1/2-inch **BLACK** squares on the corners of the unit. Draw diagonal lines on the squares; stitch, trim, and press. At this point the star center unit should measure 6-1/2-inches square.

*Make 1
star center*

Step 11 The pumpkin corner blocks are made in the same manner as the Step 10 star center. Position a 1-1/2-inch **DARK GREEN** square on the upper left corner of a 2-1/2 x 6-1/2-inch **ORANGE FLORAL** rectangle. Draw a diagonal line on the square; stitch, trim, and press. Repeat this process at the adjacent corner of the rectangle. Repeat this process at the lower corners of the rectangle using 1-1/2-inch **ORANGE PUMPKIN PRINT** squares. Make 4 units. Sew 2-1/2 x 6-1/2-inch **ORANGE PUMPKIN PRINT** rectangles to both side edges of the unit; press. Position 1-1/2-inch **BLACK** squares on the corners of the unit, draw diagonal lines on the squares; stitch, trim, and press. At this point each pumpkin unit should measure 6-1/2-inches square.

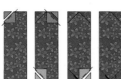

Make 4   *Make 4 pumpkin
units (set aside)*

Step 12 With right sides together, position a 3-1/2-inch **ORANGE PRINT** square on the corner of a 3-1/2 x 6-1/2-inch **BLACK** rectangle. Draw a diagonal line on the square; stitch, trim, and press. Repeat this process at the opposite corner of the rectangle.

*Make 3
star point units*

Step 13 Sew Step 12 star point units to the side edges of the Step 10 star center unit; press. Sew 3-1/2-inch **BLACK** squares to the side edges of the remaining star point unit; press. Sew this unit to the top edge of the star center unit; press. Sew 1-1/2 x 9-1/2-inch **BLACK** rectangles to the side edges of the star unit; press. At this point the star unit should measure 9-1/2 x 14-1/2-inches.

Step 14 Referring to the quilt diagram sew the Step 13 star unit to the top edge of the Step 9 roof/house unit and sew the 3-1/2 x 14-1/2-inch **DARK GREEN** rectangle to the bottom edge; press. At this point the quilt center should measure 14-1/2 x 29-1/2-inches.

Step 15 With right sides together, position a 3-1/2-inch **DARK GREEN** square on the corner of a 3-1/2 x 5-1/2-inch **BLACK** rectangle. Draw a diagonal line on the square; stitch, trim, and press. Make another unit reversing the direction of the diagonal sewing line.

Make 1   *Make 1*

Step 16 Referring to the quilt diagram, sew a 5-1/2 x 26-1/2-inch **BLACK** rectangle to the top edge of each Step 15 unit; press to make the appliqué foundation rectangles. <u>At this point each appliqué foundation rectangle should measure 5-1/2 x 29-1/2-inches.</u>

Appliqué

Cutting the Vine Strips

From **DARK GREEN PRINT:**

- Cut enough 1-3/8-inch **bias** strips to make 2, 34-inch long strips. Diagonally piece the strips together to get the length needed.

Prepare the Vine Strips

Fold each 1-3/8-inch wide **DARK GREEN** strip in half lengthwise with wrong sides together; press. To keep the raw edges aligned, stitch a scant 1/4-inch away from the edges. Fold the strip in half again so the raw edges are hidden by the first folded edge; press. Hand baste if needed. Set the vine strips aside.

Fusible Web Appliqué Method

Step 1 Make templates using the leaf and berry shapes on page 102. Trace the shapes on the paper side of the fusible web, leaving a small margin between each shape. Cut the shapes apart.

Note: *When you are fusing a large shape like the leaf, fuse just the outer edges of the shape so that it will not look stiff when finished. To do this, draw a line about 3/8-inch inside the leaf and cut away the fusible web on this line.*

Step 2 Following the manufacturer's instructions, fuse the shapes to the wrong side of the fabric chosen for the appliqués. Let the fabric cool and cut along the traced line. Peel away the paper backing from the fusible web.

Step 3 Referring to the quilt diagram, position the prepared vines and the appliqué shapes on the Step 15 appliqué foundation rectangles; hand baste or pin in place. Appliqué the vine in place; trim the ends if needed. Appliqué the leaf and berry shapes in place.

Note: *We suggest pinning a square of tear-away stabilizer to the backside of the quilt top (behind the appliqué shapes) so it will lay flat when the machine appliqué is complete.*

Step 4 We machine blanket stitched around the leaf and berry shapes using black thread. You could hand blanket stitch around the shapes with pearl cotton.

blanket stitch

Step 5 Sew the appliquéd borders to the side edges of the quilt center; press.

Step 6 Attach the 1-1/2 x 24-1/2-inch **BLACK** border strips to the top/bottom edges of the quilt center; press. <u>At this point the quilt center should measure 24-1/2 x 31-1/2-inches.</u>

Borders

Note: *The yardage given allows for the border strips to be cut on the crosswise grain. Diagonally piece the strips as needed, referring to **Diagonal Piecing** instructions on page 123. Read through **Border** instructions on page 121, for general instructions on adding borders.*

Cutting

From **BARN RED PRINT:**

- Cut 4, 1-1/2 x 42-inch inner border strips

From **BLACK PRINT:**

- Cut 2, 3-1/2 x 42-inch strips
- Cut 2, 2-1/2 x 42-inch strips
- Cut 1 more 2-1/2 x 42-inch strip.

From the strip cut:

    4, 2-1/2 x 3-1/2-inch rectangles

    4, 2-1/2-inch squares

    4, 1-1/2-inch squares

- Cut 3, 1-1/2 x 42-inch strips.

    From the strips cut:

    76, 1-1/2-inch squares

From **TAN FLORAL:**

- Cut 7, 2-1/2 x 42-inch strips. From the strips cut:

    38, 2-1/2 x 6-1/2-inch rectangles

- Cut 2, 1-1/2 x 42-inch strips

From **DARK GREEN PRINT:**

- Cut 5, 4-1/2 x 42-inch outer border strips
- Cut 1, 1-1/2 x 42-inch strip. From the strip cut:

    4, 1-1/2 x 2-1/2-inch rectangles

    8, 1-1/2-inch squares

Assembling and Attaching the Borders

Step 1   Attach the 1-1/2-inch wide **BARN RED** inner border strips.

Step 2   Aligning long edges, sew a 2-1/2 x 42-inch **BLACK** strip and a 3-1/2 x 42-inch **BLACK** strip to both side edges of a 1-1/2 x 42-inch **TAN FLORAL** strip. Press the seam allowances toward the **BLACK** strips, referring to *Hints and Helps for Pressing Strip Sets*. Make 2 strip sets. Cut the strip sets into segments.

Crosscut 34, 1-1/2-inch wide picket fence segments

Hints and Helps for Pressing Strip Sets

When sewing strips of fabric together for strip sets, it is important to press the seam allowances nice and flat, usually to the dark fabric. Be careful not to stretch as you press, causing a "rainbow effect." This will affect the accuracy and shape of the pieces cut from the strip set. I like to press on the wrong side first and with the strips perpendicular to

the ironing board. Then I flip the piece over and press on the right side to prevent little pleats from forming at the seams. Laying the strip set lengthwise on the ironing board seems to encourage the rainbow effect, as shown in diagram.

Avoid this rainbow effect

Step 3   With right sides together, position a 1-1/2-inch **BLACK** square on the upper left corner of a 2-1/2 x 6-1/2-inch **TAN FLORAL** rectangle. Draw a diagonal line on the square; stitch, trim, and press. Repeat this process at the upper right corner of the rectangle.

Make 38

Step 4   For the top/bottom picket fence border strips, sew together 8 of the Step 2 segments and 9 of the Step 3 units; press. <u>At this point each picket fence border strip should measure 6-1/2 x 26-1/2-inches.</u> Sew the picket fence border strips to the quilt center; press.

Step 5   For the side picket fence border strips, sew together 9 of the Step 2 segments and 10 of the Step 3 units; press. <u>At this point each picket fence border strip should measure 6-1/2 x 29-1/2-inches.</u> Set the side picket fence border strips aside.

Step 6   With right sides together, position a 1-1/2-inch **DARK GREEN** square on the upper left corner of a 2-1/2 x 3-1/2-inch **BLACK** rectangle. Draw a diagonal line on the square; stitch, trim, and press. Repeat this process at the upper right corner of the rectangle.

Make 4

Step 7 With right sides together, position a 1-1/2-inch **BLACK** square on the left corner of a 1-1/2 x 2-1/2-inch **DARK GREEN** rectangle. Draw a diagonal line on the square; stitch, trim, and press. Make 4 units. Sew a 2-1/2-inch **BLACK** square to each of the units; press.

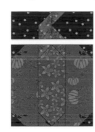

Make 4

Step 8 Sew together the Step 6 and 7 units to make the stem units; press. Sew the stem units to the pumpkin units previously made; press. Referring to the quilt diagram, sew the pumpkin blocks to the side picket fence border strips; press. Sew the border strips to the quilt center; press.

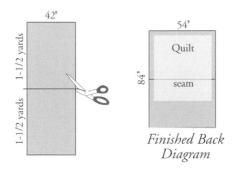

Make 4

Step 9 Attach the 4-1/2-inch wide **DARK GREEN** outer border strips.

Putting It All Together

Cut the 3 yard length of backing fabric in half crosswise to make 2, 1-1/2 yard lengths. Refer to *Finishing the Quilt* on page 123 for complete instructions.

Finished Back Diagram

Quilting Suggestions:

- Quilt center - meander.
- Leaves, fence posts, 4 side pumpkins - echo.
- **GREEN** outer border - **TB28 Leaf Sketch**.

(3")

TB28 Leaf Sketch Quilting Suggestion

THIMBLEBERRIES® quilt stencils by Quilting Creations International are available at your local quilt shop.

Binding

Cutting

From **BARN RED PRINT:**

- Cut 6, 2-3/4 x 42-inch strips

Sew the binding to the quilt using a 3/8-inch seam allowance. This measurement will produce a 1/2-inch wide finished double binding. Refer to *Binding* and *Diagonal Piecing* on page 123 for complete instructions.

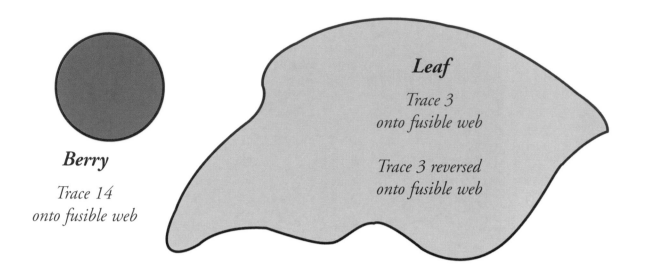

Berry

*Trace 14
onto fusible web*

Leaf

*Trace 3
onto fusible web*

*Trace 3 reversed
onto fusible web*

Pumpkin House

Wall Quilt

46 x 53-inches

Fabrics and Supplies

2-1/4 yards **TAN PRINT**
for Log Cabin strips

5/8 yard **RED PRINT** for Log Cabin
center squares and corner squares

1/3 yard **DARK GOLD PRINT**
for Log Cabin strips

1/2 yard **BLACK w/GOLD LEAF
PRINT** for Log Cabin strips

5/8 yard **RED w/GREEN LEAF PRINT**
for Log Cabin strips

5/8 yard **BROWN/GREEN LEAF
PRINT** for Log Cabin strips

1/3 yard **MEDIUM GREEN PRINT**
for Log Cabin strips

1/2 yard **BLACK/BROWN PRINT**
for Log Cabin strips

5/8 yard **GREEN w/GOLD
LEAF PRINT** for Log Cabin strips

5/8 yard **BROWN PRINT**
for Log Cabin strips

7/8 yard **LIGHT GREEN PRINT**
for narrow inner and middle borders

2 yards **SMALL VINE PRINT**
for wide middle border

2-1/2 yards **CHESTNUT PRINT**
for outer border

1 yard **BLACK/BROWN PRINT**
for binding

8-5/8 yards for backing

Quilt batting, at least 100 x 118-inches

*Before beginning this project, read through
General Instructions on page 110.*

Chevron Log Cabin

Quilt

94 x 112-inches

*An evening under the stars starts with a
harvest table topped with an impressive
Chevron Log Cabin Quilt to celebrate with
patchwork by candlelight. Traditional Log
Cabin blocks feature red center squares
as reminders of the warmth from the
embers glowing in the fireplace or the light
from the candle in the cabin window.*

Log Cabin Blocks

Block A

Makes 24 A Blocks

Cutting

From **TAN PRINT**:
- Cut 2, 2-1/2 x 42-inch strips
- Cut 13 more 2-1/2 x 42-inch strips

From **RED PRINT**:
- Cut 2, 2-1/2 x 42-inch strips

From **DARK GOLD PRINT**:
- Cut 3, 2-1/2 x 42-inch strips

From **BLACK w/GOLD LEAF PRINT**:
- Cut 5, 2-1/2 x 42-inch strips

From **RED w/GREEN LEAF PRINT**:
- Cut 6, 2-1/2 x 42-inch strips

From **BROWN/GREEN LEAF PRINT**:
- Cut 7, 2-1/2 x 42-inch strips

Piecing

Step 1 Aligning long raw edges, sew together 2 of the 2-1/2 x 42-inch **TAN** and **RED** strips in pairs. Make 2 strip sets. Press the strip sets referring to **Hints and Helps for Pressing Strip Sets**. Cut the strip sets into segments.

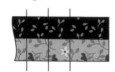

Crosscut 24, 2-1/2-inch wide segments

Hints and Helps for Pressing Strip Sets

When sewing strips of fabric together for strip sets, it is important to press the seam allowances nice and flat, usually to the dark fabric. Be careful not to stretch as you press, causing a "rainbow effect." This will affect the accuracy and shape of the pieces cut from the strip set. Press on the wrong side first with the strips perpendicular to the ironing board. Flip the piece over and press on the right side to prevent little pleats from forming at the seams. Laying the strip set lengthwise on the ironing board seems to encourage the rainbow effect.

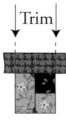

Avoid this effect

Step 2 Sew a 2-1/2-inch wide **TAN** strip to the left edge of the 2-piece unit; press. Trim the strip even with the edges of the 2-piece unit.

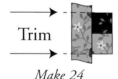

Make 24

Step 3 Sew a 2-1/2-inch wide **DARK GOLD** strip to the top edge of the unit; press and trim.

Make 24

Step 4 Sew a 2-1/2-inch wide **BLACK w/GOLD LEAF PRINT** strip to the right edge of the unit; press and trim.

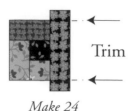

Make 24

Step 5 Working clockwise around the 2-piece unit and referring to the block diagram for color placement, continue adding the 2-1/2-inch wide **TAN** strips, **RED w/GREEN LEAF PRINT** strips, and **BROWN/GREEN LEAF PRINT** strips; press and trim after adding each strip. <u>At this point each Log Cabin block should measure 10-1/2-inches square.</u>

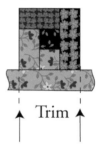

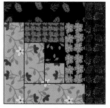

Block A
Make 24

Block B
Makes 24 B Blocks

Cutting

From **TAN PRINT**:
- Cut 2, 2-1/2 x 42-inch strips
- Cut 13 more 2-1/2 x 42-inch strips

From **RED PRINT**:
- Cut 2, 2-1/2 x 42-inch strips

From **MEDIUM GREEN PRINT**:
- Cut 3, 2-1/2 x 42-inch strips

From **BLACK/BROWN PRINT**:
- Cut 5, 2-1/2 x 42-inch strips

From **GREEN w/GOLD LEAF PRINT**:
- Cut 6, 2-1/2 x 42-inch strips

From **BROWN PRINT**:
- Cut 7, 2-1/2 x 42-inch strips

Piecing

Step 1 Aligning long raw edges, sew together 2 of the 2-1/2 x 42-inch **TAN** and **RED** strips in pairs; press. Make 2 strip sets. Cut the strip sets into segments.

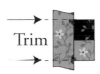

Crosscut 24, 2-1/2-inch wide segments

Step 2 Sew a 2-1/2-inch wide **TAN** strip to the left edge of the 2-piece unit; press and trim.

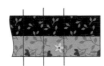

Make 24

Step 3 Sew a 2-1/2-inch wide **MEDIUM GREEN** strip to the top edge of the unit; press and trim.

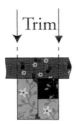

Make 24

Step 4 Sew a 2-1/2-inch wide **BLACK/BROWN PRINT** strip to the right edge of the unit; press and trim.

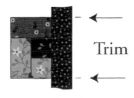

Make 24

Step 5 Working clockwise around the 2-piece unit and referring to the block diagram for color placement,

continue adding the 2-1/2-inch wide **TAN** strips, **GREEN w/GOLD LEAF PRINT** strips, and **BROWN PRINT** strips; press and trim after adding each strip. At this point each Log Cabin block should measure 10-1/2-inches square.

Block B
Make 24

Quilt Center Assembly

Step 1 Referring to the quilt diagram for block placement, lay out the A and B blocks in 8 rows with 6 blocks in each row. Sew the blocks together in each row. Press the seam allowances in alternating directions by rows so the seams will fit snugly together with less bulk.

Step 2 Pin the rows together at the block intersections; stitch. At this point the quilt center should measure 60-1/2 x 80-1/2-inches.

Borders

Note: *The yardage given allows for the border strips to be cut on the crosswise grain. Piece the **SMALL VINE PRINT** wide middle border strips on the straight of grain; the vines will be easier to match. Diagonally piece the remaining border strips together, referring to **Diagonal Piecing** on page 123 for complete instructions. Read through **Border** instructions on page 121 for general instructions on adding borders.*

Cutting

From **LIGHT GREEN PRINT**:
- Cut 18, 1-1/2 x 42-inch narrow inner and middle border strips

From **SMALL VINE PRINT**:
- Cut 8, 7-1/2 x 42-inch wide middle border strips - piece on the straight of grain

From **CHESTNUT PRINT**:
- Cut 11, 7-1/2 x 42-inch outer border strips

From **RED PRINT**:
- Cut 1, 8-1/2 x 42-inch strip. From the strip cut: 4, 8-1/2-inch corner squares

Attaching the Borders

Step 1 For the top/bottom borders, measure the quilt from left to right through the middle. Cut 2, 1-1/2-inch wide **LIGHT GREEN** strips and 2, 7-1/2-inch wide **SMALL VINE PRINT** strips to the length needed (plus a few extra inches for trimming). Referring to the quilt diagram, sew the **LIGHT GREEN** and **SMALL VINE PRINT** strips together in pairs; press. Attach the top/bottom pieced border strips; press and trim.

Step 2 For the side borders, measure just the quilt from top to bottom including the seam allowances, but not the top/bottom borders just added. Cut 2, 1-1/2-inch wide **LIGHT GREEN** strips and 2, 7-1/2-inch wide **SMALL VINE PRINT** strips to this length. Sew the **LIGHT GREEN** and **SMALL VINE PRINT** strips together in pairs; press. Sew the 8-1/2-inch **RED** corner squares to both ends of the pieced border strips. Sew the pieced border strips to the side edges of the quilt center.

Step 3 Attach the 1-1/2-inch wide **LIGHT GREEN** narrow middle border strips.

Step 4 Attach the 7-1/2-inch wide **CHESTNUT** outer border strips.

Putting It All Together

Cut the 8-5/8 yard length of backing fabric in thirds crosswise to make 3, 2-7/8 yard lengths. Refer to *Finishing the Quilt* on page 123 for complete instructions.

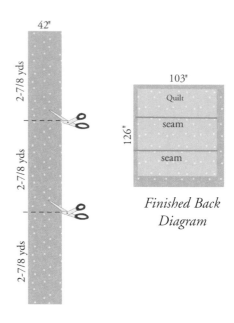

Finished Back Diagram

Quilting Suggestions:

- Light area of quilt center - feathered vines.

- Dark area of quilt center - large meander.

- **SMALL VINE PRINT** middle border - crosshatching.

- **RED** corner square - feathered wreath.

- **CHESTNUT** outer border - feathered vines and channel stitching.

Binding

Cutting

From **BLACK/BROWN PRINT**:
- Cut 11, 2-3/4 x 42-inch strips

Sew the binding to the quilt using a 3/8-inch seam allowance. This measurement will produce a 1/2-inch wide finished double binding. Refer to *Binding* and *Diagonal Piecing* on page 123 for complete instructions.

Chevron Log Cabin

Quilt

94 x 112-inches

General Instructions & Glossary

Yardage is based on 42-inch wide fabric. If your fabric is wider or narrower, it will affect the amount of necessary strips you need to cut in some patterns, and of course, it will affect the amount of fabric you have left over. Generally, Thimbleberries® patterns allow for a little extra fabric so you can confidently cut your pattern pieces with ease.

A rotary cutter, mat, and wide clear acrylic ruler with 1/8-inch markings are needed tools in attaining accuracy. A beginner needs good tools just as an experienced quiltmaker needs good equipment. A 24 x 36-inch cutting mat is a good size to own. It will easily accommodate the average quilt fabrics and will aid in accurate cutting. The acrylic ruler you purchase should be at least 6 x 24-inches and easy to read. Do not purchase a smaller ruler to save money. The large size will be invaluable to your quiltmaking success.

It is often recommended to prewash and press fabrics to test for colorfastness and possible shrinkage. If you choose to prewash, wash in cool water and dry in a cool to moderate dryer. Industry standards actually suggest that line drying is best. Shrinkage is generally very minimal and usually is not a concern. A good way to test your fabric for both shrinkage and colorfastness is to cut a 3-inch square of fabric. Soak the fabric in a white bowl filled with water. Squeeze the water out of the fabric and press it dry on a piece of muslin. If the fabric is going to release color, it will do so either in the water or when it is pressed dry. Remeasure the 3-inch fabric square to see if it has changed size considerably (more than 1/4-inch). If it has, wash, dry, and press the entire yardage. This little test could save you hours in prewashing and pressing.

Read instructions thoroughly before beginning a project. Each step will make more sense to you when you have a general overview of the whole process. Take one step at a time and follow the illustrations. They will often make more sense to you than the words. Take "baby steps" so you don't get overwhelmed by the entire process.

When working with flannel and other loosely woven fabrics, always prewash and dry. These fabrics almost always shrink more.

For piecing, place right sides of the fabric pieces together and use 1/4-inch seam allowances throughout the entire quilt unless otherwise specifically stated in the directions. An accurate seam allowance is the most important part of the quiltmaking process after accurately cutting. All the directions are based on accurate 1/4-inch seam allowances. It is very important to check your sewing machine to see what position your fabric should be to get accurate seams.

To test, use a piece of 1/4-inch graph paper, stitch along the quarter inch line as if the paper were fabric. Make note of where the edge of the paper lines up with your presser foot or where it lines up on the throat plate of your machine. Many quilters place a piece of masking tape on the throat plate to help guide the edge of the fabric. Now test your seam allowance on fabric. Cut 2, 2-1/2-inch squares, place right sides together and stitch along one edge. Press seam allowances in one direction and measure. At this point the unit should measure 2-1/2 x 4-1/2-inches. If it does not, adjust your stitching guidelines and test again. Seam allowances are included in the cutting sizes given in this book.

Pressing is the third most important step in quiltmaking. As a general rule, you should never cross a stitched seam with another seam unless it has been pressed. Therefore, every time you stitch a seam, it needs to be pressed before adding another piece. Often, it will feel like you press as much as you sew, and often that is true. It is very important that you press and not iron the seams. Pressing is a firm, up-and-down motion that will flatten the seams but not distort the piecing. Ironing is a back-and-forth motion and will stretch and distort the small pieces. Most quilters use steam to help the pressing process. The moisture does help and will not distort the shapes as long as the pressing motion is used.

An old-fashioned rule is to press seam allowances in one direction, toward the darker fabric. Often, background fabrics are light in color and pressing toward the darker fabric prevents the seam allowances from showing through to the right side. Pressing seam allowances in one direction is thought to create a stronger seam. Also, for ease in hand quilting, the quilting lines should fall on the side of the seam which is opposite the seam allowance. As you piece quilts, you will find these "rules" to be helpful but not neccesarily always appropriate. Sometimes seams need to be pressed in the opposite direction so the seams of different units will fit together more easily, which quilters refer to as seams "nesting" together. When sewing together two units with opposing seam allowances, use the tip of your seam ripper to gently guide the units under your presser foot. Sometimes it is necessary to re-press the seams to make the units fit together nicely. Always try to achieve the least bulk in one spot and accept that no matter which way you press, it may be a little tricky and it could be a little bulky.

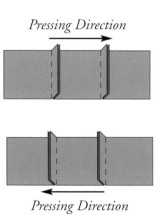

Pressing Direction

Pressing Direction

Squaring Up Blocks

To square up your blocks, first check the seam allowances. This is usually where the problem is, and it is always best to alter within the block rather than trim the outer edges. Next, make sure you have pressed accurately. Sometimes a block can become distorted by ironing instead of pressing.

To trim up block edges, use one of the many clear acrylic squares available on the market. Determine the center of the block; mark with a pin. Lay the square over the block and align as many perpendicular and horizontal lines as you can to the seams in your block. This will indicate where the block is off.

Do not trim all off on one side; this usually results in real distortion of the pieces in the block and the block design. Take a little fabric off all sides until the block is square. When assembling many blocks, it is necessary to make sure all are the same size.

Tools and Equipment

Making beautiful quilts does not require a large number of specialized tools or expensive equipment. My list of favorites is short and sweet and includes the things I use over and over again because they are always accurate and dependable.

I find a long acrylic ruler indispensable for accurate rotary cutting. The ones I like most are an Omnigrid® 6 x 24-inch grid acrylic ruler for cutting long strips and squaring up fabrics and quilt tops and a MasterPiece® 45-degree (8 x 24-inch) ruler for cutting 6- to 8-inch wide borders. I sometimes tape together two 6 x 24-inch acrylic rulers for cutting borders up to 12-inches wide.

A 15-inch Omnigrid® square acrylic ruler is great for squaring up individual blocks and corners of a quilt top, for cutting strips up to 15-inches wide or long, and for trimming side and corner triangles.

I think the markings on my 24 x 36-inch Olfa® rotary cutting mat stay visible longer than on other mats, and the lines are fine and accurate.

The largest size Olfa® rotary cutter cuts through many layers of fabric easily, and isn't cumbersome to use. The 2-1/2-inch blade slices through three layers of backing, batting, and a quilt top like butter.

An 8-inch pair of Gingher shears is great for cutting out appliqué templates and cutting fabric from a bolt or fabric scraps.

I keep a pair of 5-1/2-inch Gingher scissors by my sewing machine so it is handy for both machine work and handwork. This size is versatile and sharp enough to make large and small cuts equally well.

My Grabbit® magnetic pincushion has a surface that is large enough to hold lots of straight pins and a magnet strong enough to keep them securely in place.

Silk pins are long and thin, which means they won't leave large holes in your fabric. I like them because they increase accuracy in pinning pieces or blocks together. It is also easy to press over silk pins.

For pressing individual pieces, blocks, and quilt tops, I use an 18 x 48-inch sheet of plywood covered with several layers of cotton fiberfill and topped with a layer of muslin stapled to the back. The 48-inch length allows me to press an entire width of fabric at one time without the need to reposition it, and the square ends are better than tapered ends on an ironing board for pressing finished quilt tops.

Using Grain

The fabric you purchase still has selvage and before beginning to handle or cut your fabric, it's helpful to be able to recognize and understand its basic characteristics. Fabric is produced in the mill with identifiable grain or direction. These are: lengthwise, crosswise and bias.

The lengthwise grain is the direction that fabric comes off the milling machine, and is parallel to the selvage. This grain of the fabric has the least stretch and the greatest strength.

The crosswise grain is the short distance that spans a bolt's 42-inch to 44-inch width. The crosswise grain, or width of grain, is between two sides called selvages. This grain of the fabric has medium stretch and medium strength.

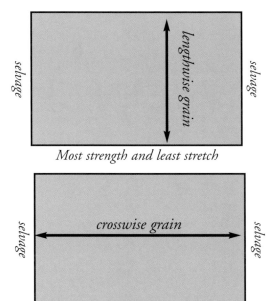

Most strength and least stretch

Medium strength and medium stretch

Avoiding Bias

The 45-degree angle on a piece of fabric is the bias and the direction with the most stretch. I suggest avoiding sewing on the bias until you're confident handling fabric. With practice and careful handling, bias edges can be sewn and are best for making curves.

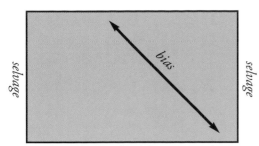

Least strength and most stretch

Rotary Cutting

SAFETY FIRST! The blades of a rotary cutter are very sharp and need to be for accurate cutting. Look at a variety of cutters to find one that feels good in your hand. All quality cutters have a safety mechanism to "close" the cutting blade when not in use. After each cut and before laying the rotary cutter down, close the blade. Soon this will become second nature to you and will prevent dangerous accidents. Always keep cutters out of the sight of children. Rotary cutters are very tempting to fiddle with when they are laying around. When your blade is dull or nicked, change it. Damaged blades do not cut accurately and require extra effort that can also result in slipping and injury. Also, always cut away from yourself for safety.

Squaring Off Fabric

Fold the fabric in half lengthwise matching the selvage edges.

Square off the ends of your fabric before measuring and cutting pieces. This means that the cut edge of the fabric must be exactly perpendicular to the folded edge which creates a 90-degree angle. Align the folded and selvage edges of the fabric with the lines on the cutting board, and place a ruled square on the fold. Place a 6 x 24-inch ruler against the side of the square to get a 90-degree angle. Hold the ruler in place, remove the square, and cut along the edge of the ruler. If you are left-handed, work from the other end of the fabric. Use the lines on your cutting board to help line up fabric, but not to measure and cut strips. Use a ruler for accurate cutting, always checking to make sure your fabric is lined up with horizontal and vertical lines on the ruler.

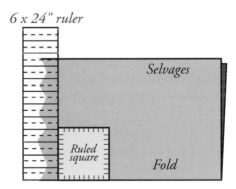

6 x 24" ruler
Selvages
Ruled square
Fold

Cutting Strips

When cutting strips or rectangles, cut on the crosswise grain. Strips can then be cut into squares or smaller rectangles.

If your strips are not straight after cutting a few of them, refold the fabric, align the folded and selvage edges with the lines on the cutting board, and "square off" the edge again by trimming to straighten, and begin cutting.

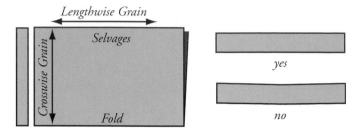

Cutting Bias Strips

When cutting bias strips, trim your yardage on the crosswise grain so the edges are straight. With right sides facing up, fold the yardage on the diagonal. Fold the selvage edge (lengthwise grain) over to meet the cut edge (crosswise grain), forming a triangle. This diagonal fold is the true bias. Position the ruler to the desired strip width from the cut edge and cut one strip. Continue moving the ruler across the fabric cutting parallel strips in the desired widths.

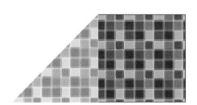

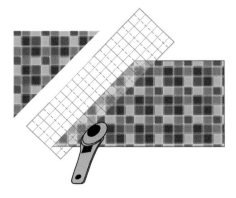

Trimming Side and Corner Triangles

In projects with side and corner triangles, the instructions have you cut side and corner triangles larger than needed. This will allow you to square up the quilt and eliminates the frustration of ending up with pre-cut side and corner triangles that don't match the size of your pieced blocks.

To cut triangles, first cut squares. The project directions will tell you what size to make the squares and whether to cut them in half to make two triangles or to cut them in quarters to make four triangles, as shown in the diagrams. This cutting method will give you side triangles that have the straight grain on the outside edges of the quilt. This is a very important part of quiltmaking that will help stabilize your quilt center.

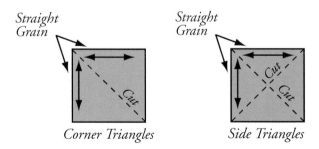

Corner Triangles   Side Triangles

Helpful Hints for Sewing with Flannel

Always prewash and machine dry flannel. This will prevent severe shrinkage after the quilt is made. Some flannels shrink more than others. For this reason, we have allowed approximately 1/4 yard extra for each fabric under the fabric requirements. Treat the more heavily napped side of solid flannels as the right side of the fabric.

Because flannel stretches more than other cotton calicos and because the nap makes them thicker, the quilt design should be simple. Let the fabric and color make the design statement.

Consider combining regular cotton calicos with flannels. The different textures complement each other nicely.

Use a 10 to 12 stitches per inch setting on your machine. A 1/4-inch seam allowance is also recommended for flannel piecing.

When sewing triangle-pieced squares together, take extra care not to stretch the diagonal seam. Trim off the points from the seam allowances to eliminate bulk.

Press gently to prevent stretching pieces out of shape.

Check block measurements as you progress. "Square up" the blocks as needed. Flannel will shift and it is easy to end up with blocks that are misshapen. If you trim and measure as you go, you are more likely to have accurate blocks. If you notice a piece of flannel is stretching more than the others, place it on the bottom when stitching on the

machine. The natural action of the feed dogs will help prevent it from stretching.

Before stitching pieces, strips, or borders together, pin often to prevent fabric from stretching and moving. When stitching longer pieces together, divide the pieces into quarters and pin. Divide into even smaller sections to get more control.

Use a lightweight batting to prevent the quilt from becoming too heavy.

Cutting Triangles from Squares

Cutting accurate triangles can be intimidating for beginners, but a clear acrylic ruler, rotary cutter, and cutting mat are all that are needed to make perfect triangles. The cutting instructions often direct you to cut strips, then squares, and then triangles.

Sewing Layered Strips Together

When you are instructed to layer strips, right sides together, and sew, you need to take some precautions. Gently lay one strip on top of another, carefully lining up the raw edges. Pressing the strips together will hold them together nicely, and a few pins here and there will also help. Be careful not to stretch the strips as you sew them together.

Rod Casing or Sleeve to Hang Quilts

To hang wall quilts, attach a casing that is made of the same fabric as the quilt back. Attach this casing at the top of the quilt, just below the binding. Often, it is helpful to attach a second casing at the bottom of the quilt so you can insert a dowel into it which will help weight the quilt and make it hang free of ripples.

To make a rod casing or "sleeve," cut enough strips of fabric equal to the width of the quilt plus 2-inches for side hems. Generally, 6-inch wide strips will accommodate most rods. If you are using a rod with a larger diameter, increase the width of the strips.

Seam the strips together to get the length needed; press. Fold the strip in half lengthwise, wrong sides together. Stitch the long raw edges together with a 1/4-inch seam allowance. Center the seam on the backside of the sleeve; press. The raw edges of the seam will be concealed when the sleeve is stitched to the back of the quilt. Turn under both of the short raw edges; press and stitch to hem the ends. The final measurement should be about 1/2-inch from the quilt edges.

Pin the sleeve to the back of the quilt so the top edge of the sleeve is just below the binding. Hand stitch the top edge of the sleeve in place, then the bottom edge. Make sure to knot and secure your stitches at each end of the sleeve to make sure it will not pull away from the quilt with use. Slip the rod into the casing. If your wall quilt is not directional, making a sleeve for the bottom edge will allow you to turn your quilt end to end to relieve the stress at the top edge. You could also slip a dowel into the bottom sleeve to help anchor the lower edge of the wall quilt.

Hand stitch the sleeve to the quilt back

Choosing a Quilting Design

Quilting is such an individual process that it is difficult to recommend designs for each quilt. There are hundreds of quilting stencils available at quilt shops. (Templates are used generally for appliqué shapes; stencils are used for marking quilting designs.) I have developed several Thimbleberries® Quilt Stencils for Quilting Creations that are appropriate for hand quilting and continuous machine quilting.

There are a few suggestions that may help you decide how to quilt your project, depending on how much time you would like to spend quilting. Many quilters now use professional longarm quilting machines or hire someone skilled at running these machines to do the quilting. This, of course, frees up more time to piece quilt tops.

- OUTLINE QUILTING
  follows the outline and accentuates a pieced or appliquéd block by stitching about 1/4-inch away from the seam line or edge of the appliqué shape. It requires no marking. This can be done by hand or machine.

- IN-THE-DITCH QUILTING
  is understated because it nearly disappears in the seam. The stitches are made next to the seam line or along an appliqué edge. It requires no marking and is a good choice for machine quilting or hand quilting.

- BACKGROUND QUILTING
  (crosshatch or grid design) fills large spaces and puts more emphasis on the quilt patterns by making them stand out from the background. Background quilting can be done in straight lines or in a random pattern. This can be done by hand or machine.

- STIPPLE QUILTING (meandering)
  requires no marking to create the random curves that flow across a quilt surface or fill areas of a quilt (that may already have a design) with concentrated quilting stitches. The goal is to avoid having the stitches cross over one another. This is rarely done by hand.

- DESIGN QUILTING
  is often a decorative accent in its own right. Popular designs include feathers, wreaths, cables, and swags which work well in open spaces such as large corner blocks or borders. This can be done by hand or machine.

- ECHO QUILTING
  highlights a motif—usually an appliqué piece. Once the motif is outlined, two or three parallel rows of stitching are added at regular intervals. This can be done by hand or machine.

Quilting Suggestions

Repeat one of the design elements in the quilt as part of the quilting design.

Two or three parallel rows of echo quilting outside an appliqué piece will highlight the shape.

Stipple or meander quilting behind a feather or central motif will make the primary design more prominent.

Look for quilting designs that will cover two or more borders, rather than choosing separate designs for each individual border.

Quilting in-the-ditch of seams is an effective way to get a project quilted without a great deal of time marking the quilt.

Outline Quilting   **In-the-Ditch Quilting**   **Background Quilting**

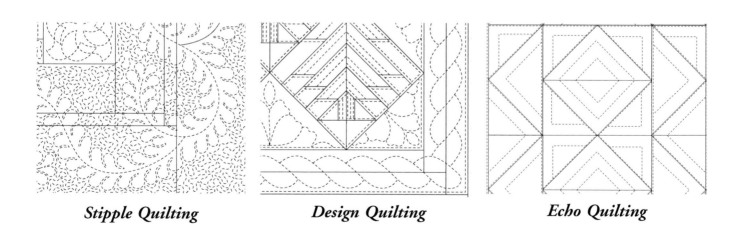

Stipple Quilting   **Design Quilting**   **Echo Quilting**

Marking the Quilting Design

When marking the quilt top, use a marking tool that will be visible on the quilt fabric and yet will be easy enough to remove. Always test your marking tool on a scrap of fabric before marking the entire quilt.

Along with a multitude of commercial marking tools available, you may find that very thin slivers of hand soap (Dial, Ivory, etc.) work well for marking medium to dark color fabrics. The thin lines of soap show up nicely and they are easily removed by simply rubbing gently with a piece of like-colored fabric.

Hints and Helps for Pressing Strip Sets

When sewing strips of fabric together for strip sets, it is important to press the seam allowances nice and flat, usually to the darker fabric. Be careful not to stretch as you press, causing a "rainbow effect." This will affect the accuracy and shape of the pieces cut from the strip set. I like to press on the wrong side first and with the strips perpendicular to the ironing board. Then I flip the piece over and press on the right side to prevent little pleats from forming at the seams. Laying the strip set lengthwise on the ironing board seems to

encourage the rainbow effect, as shown in the diagram.

Avoid this rainbow effect

Borders

NOTE: Cut borders to the width called for. Always cut border strips a few inches longer than needed, just to be safe. Diagonally piece the border strips together as needed.

1. With pins, mark the center points along all 4 sides of the quilt. For the top and bottom borders, measure the quilt from left to right through the middle.

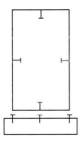

2. Measure and mark the border lengths and center points on the strips cut for the borders before sewing them on.

3. Pin the border strips to the quilt and stitch a 1/4-inch seam. Press the seam allowances toward the border. Trim off excess border lengths.

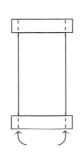

Trim away excess fabric

4. For the side borders, measure your quilt from top to bottom, including the borders just added, to determine the length of the side borders.

5. Measure and mark the side border lengths as you did for the top and bottom borders.

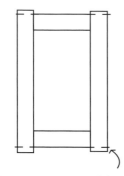

Trim away excess fabric

6. Pin and stitch the side border strips in place. Press and trim the border strips even with the borders just added.

7. If your quilt has multiple borders, measure, mark, and sew additional borders to the quilt in the same manner.

Decorative Stitches

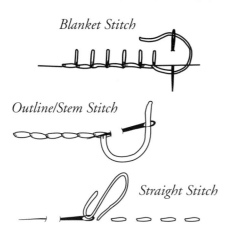

Blanket Stitch

Outline/Stem Stitch

Straight Stitch

Choosing the Backing

The backing of any quilt is just as important to the overall design as the pieced patchwork top. Combine large-scale prints or piece coordinating fabrics together to create an interesting quilt back. Using large pieces of fabric (perhaps three different prints that are the same length as the quilt) or a large piece of fabric that is bordered by compatible prints, keeps the number of seams to a minimum, which speeds up the process. The new 108-inch wide fabric sold on the bolt eliminates the need for seaming entirely. Carefully selected fabrics for a well-constructed backing not only complement a finished quilt, but make it more useful as a reversible accent.

Crib—45 x 60-inches

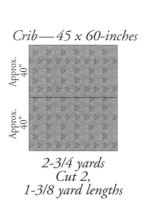

*2-3/4 yards
Cut 2,
1-3/8 yard lengths*

Twin—72 x 90-inches

Approx. 40"   Approx. 40"
*5-1/3 yards
Cut 2, 2-2/3 yard lengths*

Double/Full—81 x 96-inches

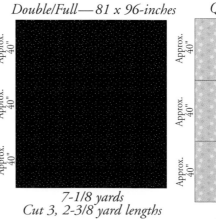

*7-1/8 yards
Cut 3, 2-3/8 yard lengths*

Queen—90 x 108-inches

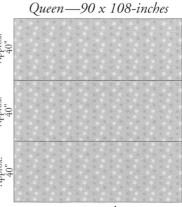

*8 yards
Cut 3, 2-2/3 yard lengths*

Finishing the Quilt

1. Remove the selvages from the backing fabric. Sew the long edges together and press. Trim the backing and batting so they are 4-inches to 6-inches larger than the quilt top.

2. Mark the quilt top for quilting. Layer the backing, batting, and quilt top. Baste the 3 layers together and quilt.

3. When quilting is complete, remove basting. Hand baste all 3 layers together a scant 1/4-inch from the edge. This hand basting keeps the layers from shifting and prevents puckers from forming when adding the binding. Trim excess batting and backing fabric even with the edge of the quilt top. Add the binding as shown below.

Binding and Diagonal Piecing

1. Diagonally piece the binding strips. Fold the strip in half lengthwise, wrong sides together, and press.

Diagonal Piecing

Stitch diagonally

Trim to 1/4-inch seam allowance

Press seam open

2. Unfold and trim one end at a 45-degree angle. Turn under the edge 3/8-inch and press. Refold the strip.

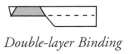

Double-layer Binding

3. With raw edges of the binding and quilt top even, stitch with a 3/8-inch seam allowance, starting 2-inches from the angled end.

4. Miter the binding at the corners. As you approach a corner of the quilt, stop sewing 3/8-inch from the corner of the quilt.

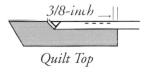

Quilt Top

5. Clip the threads and remove the quilt from under the presser foot. Flip the binding strip up and away from the quilt, then fold the binding down even with the raw edge of the quilt. Begin sewing at the upper edge. Miter all 4 corners in this manner.

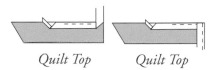

Quilt Top   *Quilt Top*

6. Trim the end of the binding so it can be tucked inside of the beginning binding about 1/2-inch. Finish stitching the seam.

Quilt Back   *Quilt Back*

7. Turn the folded edge of the binding over the raw edges and to the back of the quilt so that the stitching line does not show. Hand sew the binding in place, folding in the mitered corners as you stitch.

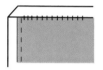 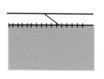

Quilt Back   *Quilt Back*   *Quilt Back*

Glossary

Appliqué The sewing technique for attaching pieces (appliqués) of fabric onto a background fabric. Appliqués may be stitched to the background by hand, using a blind stitch, or by machine, using a satin stitch or a blind hemstitch.

Backing The bottom layer of a quilt consisting of one whole piece of fabric or several fabrics joined together.

Basting The technique for joining layers of fabric or the layers of a quilt with safety pins (pin basting) or large stitches (hand basting).

The pinning or stitching is temporary and is removed after permanent stitching.

Batting A layer of filler placed between two pieces of fabric to form a quilt. Its thickness and fiber content varies.

Bias The grain of woven fabric that is at a 45-degree angle to the selvages. The bias grain has more stretch and is less stable than the crosswise or lengthwise grain.

Bias strips Strips of fabric cut on the bias and joined to make one continuous strip for binding that can easily be positioned around curved edges.

Binding The strip of fabric used to cover the outside edges—top, batting and backing— of a quilt.

Block A basic unit, usually square and often repeated, of a quilt top.

Borders The framing on a quilt that serves to visually hold in the design and give the eye a stopping point.

Crosscutting Cutting fabric strips into smaller units, such as squares or rectangles.

Crosswise grain The threads running perpendicular to the selvage across the width of a woven fabric.

Cutting mat Surface used for rotary cutting that protects the tabletop and keeps the fabric from shifting while cutting. Often mats are labeled as self-healing, meaning the blade does not leave slash marks or grooves in the surface even after repeated use.

Double-fold binding Binding made from a fabric strip that is folded in half before being attached to the quilt. Also, referred to as French-fold binding.

Finished size The measurement of a completed block or quilt.

Free-motion or machine quilting A process of quilting done with the feed dogs disengaged and using a darning presser foot so the quilt can be moved freely on the machine bed in any direction.

Grain The direction of woven fabric. The crosswise grain is from selvage to selvage. The lengthwise grain runs parallel to the selvage and is stronger. The bias grain is at a 45-degree angle and has the greatest amount of stretch.

Hand quilting Series of running stitches made through all layers of a quilt with needle and thread.

Hanging sleeve Tube of fabric that is attached to the quilt back. A wooden dowel is inserted through the fabric tube to hang the quilt. It is also called a rod pocket and used with a board or rod as a support to hang a quilt on the wall.

Inner border A strip of fabric, usually more narrow than the outer border, that frames the quilt center.

Layering Placing the quilt top, batting and quilt backing on top of each other in layers.

Lengthwise grain The threads running parallel to the selvage in a woven fabric.

Longarm quilting A quilting machine used by professional quilters in which the quilt is held taut on a frame that allows the quilter to work on a large portion of the quilt at a time. The machine head moves freely, allowing the operator to use free-motion to quilt in all directions.

Machine quilting Series of stitches made through all layers of a quilt sandwich with a sewing machine.

Marking tools A variety of pens, pencils and chalks that can be used to mark fabric pieces or a quilt top.

Mitered seam A 45-degree angle seam.

Outer border A strip of fabric that is joined to the edges of the quilt top to finish or frame it.

Pieced border Blocks or pieced units sewn together to make a single border unit that is then sewn to the quilt center.

Piecing The process of sewing pieces of fabric together.

Pressing Using an iron with an up and down motion to set stitches and flatten a seam allowance, rather than sliding it across the fabric.

Quilt center The quilt top before borders are added.

Quilt top Top layer of a quilt usually consisting of pieced blocks.

Quilting The small running stitches made through the layers of a quilt (quilt top, batting and backing) to form decorative patterns on the surface of the quilt and hold the layers together.

Quilting stencils Quilting patterns with open areas through which a design is transferred onto a quilt top. May be purchased or made from sturdy, reusable template plastic.

Rotary cutter Tool with a sharp, round blade attached to a handle that is used to cut fabric. The blade is available in different diameters.

Rotary cutting The process of cutting fabric into strips and pieces using a revolving blade

rotary cutter, a thick, clear acrylic ruler and a special cutting mat.

Running stitches A series of in-and-out stitches used in hand quilting.

Seam allowance The 1/4-inch margin of fabric between the stitched seam and the raw edge.

Selvage The lengthwise finished edge on each side of the fabric.

Slipstitch A hand stitch used for finishing such as sewing binding to a quilt where the thread is hidden by slipping the needle between a fold of fabric and tacking down with small stitches.

Squaring up or straightening fabric The process of trimming the raw edge of the fabric so it creates a 90-degree angle with the folded edge of the fabric. Squaring up is also a term used when trimming a quilt block.

Strip sets Two or more strips of fabric, cut and sewn together along the length of the strips.

Triangle-pieced square The square unit created when two 90-degree triangles are sewn together on the diagonal.

Unfinished size The measurement of a block before the 1/4-inch seam allowance is sewn or the quilt is quilted and bound.

Thimbleberries® Books by Lynette Jensen
Recent Releases

Thimbleberries® books are available at bookstores, fabric and craft stores. If you are unable to find them at your favorite retailer, contact Landauer Corporation at 1-800-557-2144 or visit www.landauercorp.com

**Thimbleberries® Quilts
for My Sister's House**
ISBN: 978-1-890621-57-5

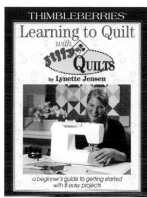

**Thimbleberries® Learning
to Quilt with Jiffy Quilts**
ISBN: 978-1-890621-51-3

**Thimbleberries®
Photo-Ready Scrapbook**
ISBN: 978-1-890621-54-4

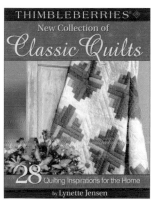

**Thimbleberries® New
Collection of Classic Quilts**
ISBN: 978-1-890621-98-8

**Thimbleberries®
Collection of Classic Quilts**
ISBN: 978-1-890621-88-9

**Thimbleberries® Four Seasons
of Calendar Table Toppers**
ISBN: 978-0-9770166-8-6

**Thimbleberries®
Quilting for Harvest**
ISBN: 978-1-890621-16-2

**Thimbleberries® Big
Book of Quilt Blocks**
ISBN: 978-1932533-05-7

**Thimbleberries®
Beginner's Luck**
ISBN: 978-0972558-01-3

**Thimbleberries®
Pint-Size Traditions**
ISBN: 978-1932533-03-3

**Thimbleberries® Oh Sew
Cozy Flannel Quilts**
ISBN: 978-1932533-04-0